# Destined to Prevail

*The dynamics of Spiritual Warfare*

# Nicky S. Raiborde

Copyright © 2008 by Nicky S. Raiborde

*Destined to Prevail*
*The dynamics of Spiritual Warfare*
by Nicky S. Raiborde

Edited by Edie Veach.

Printed in the United States of America

Library of Congress Cataloging-in-Publication Data
ISBN 978-1-60647-417-4

www.xulonpress.com

# Dedication

—☙

As we walk with God, the Holy Spirit brings people to make deposits in our life that help us reach our destiny in God, therefore I take the opportunity, as the list increases, to thank fathers, mentors, coaches, pastors, and friends who have been faithful to love, discipline, teach, and help me walk uprightly before God. "Thank you Jesus for surrounding me with people who instruct, impart, ignite, impact, and inspire my life."

**Dad and Mom** – (Instruct) Thank you for instilling in me the fear of God, helping me to hear the voice of God, and creating an atmosphere where I could answer the call of God.

**Pastor Timothy John** (Impart) –Every time I am with you, it has been a time of spiritual impartation. I have learned the importance of study, discipline, and commitment. I tried all the helps of preparing sermons and studying, but through our times together and sermons notes and outlines, I learned to study the word of God. I'm forever grateful to you.

**Br. S.R. Manohar** (Ignite)– You are a season changer. You have made me hungry for the presence and power of God. God has designed my times with you to change the seasons in my life. You totally ignite a flame of the Holy Ghost presence and power in my life and ministry.

**Jerry Horst** (Impact) - Thank you for believing in me, trusting me, and pushing me to experience God. Your input in my life through your words, shared times, lifestyle, character, and prayer are like glue that has held up everything in my life. My relationships, my behavior, and expectancy in life have totally been transformed. You have added strength to the foundation in my life.

**Johnny Lever** (Inspire) – You are a life saver. I can say, you have taught me the power of Humility. Thank you for all the times we share. Those times have shaped my preaching, my attitude, and most of all, have given me the confidence that "with God All things are possible!" You have helped me lay foundation for ministry and embrace a militant, aggressive attitude in proclaiming Jesus.

# Table of Contents

## PART IV: Satan's Weapons

## PART V: The Believer's Weapons

# PART I

# The Believer's Introduction to Warfare

# A Soldier's Confession

*I am a soldier in the army of my God.*
*The Lord Jesus Christ is my commanding officer.*
*The Holy Bible is my code of conduct;*
*Faith, prayer, and the Word are my weapons of warfare.*
*I have been taught by the Holy Spirit and God-sent people—*
*Trained by experience, tried by adversity, and tested by fire.*
*I am a volunteer in this army, and I am enlisted for eternity.*
*I will either retire in this army at the rapture or die in this army;*
*But I will not get out, sell out, be talked out, or pushed out.*
*I am faithful, reliable, capable, and dependable.*
*If my God needs me, I am there.*
*If He needs me in the Sunday school*
*To teach the children, work with the youth, help adults, or just sit*
*    and learn,*
*I'll be there.*
*He can use me because I am there!*
*I am a soldier.*
*I am not a baby.*
*I do not need to be pampered, petted, primed up, pumped up,*
*    picked up, or pepped up.*
*I am a soldier.*
*No one has to call me, remind me, write me, visit me, entice me,*
*    or lure me.*
*I am a soldier.*

*I am not a wimp.*
*I am in place—*
*Saluting my King, obeying His orders, praising His name, and*
*    building His kingdom!*
*No one has to send me flowers, gifts, food, cards, candy,*
*    or give me handouts.*
*I do not need to be cuddled, cradled, cared for, or catered to.*
*I am committed.*
*I cannot have my feelings hurt bad enough to turn me around.*
*I cannot be discouraged enough to turn me aside.*
*I cannot lose enough to cause me to quit.*
*If I end up with nothing, I will still come out ahead.*
*I will win.*
*My God has supplied and will continue to supply all of my needs.*
*I am more than a conqueror.*
*I will always triumph.*
*I can do all things through Christ.*
*Devils cannot defeat me.*
*People cannot disillusion me.*
*Weather cannot weary me.*
*Sickness cannot stop me.*
*Battles cannot beat me.*
*Money cannot buy me.*
*Governments cannot silence me, and hell cannot handle me.*
*I am a soldier.*
*Even death cannot destroy me.*
*For when my Commander calls me from this battlefield,*
*He will promote me to captain and then allow me to rule with Him.*
*I am a soldier in the army, and I'm marching, claiming victory.*
*I will not give up.*
*I will not turn around.*
*I am a soldier in the Army of God..*

~author unknown~

# Chapter 1

# Introduction

*"You therefore must endure hardship as a good soldier of Jesus Christ. No one engaged in warfare entangles himself with the affairs of this life, that he may please him who enlisted him as a soldier"* (2 Timothy 2:3–4).

You are destined to prevail! Your life may be rife with battles, but you already have been declared a conqueror. Romans 8:37 tells us, "Yet in all these things we are more than conquerors through Him who loved us."

The battles you face are a part of an all-out war between the flesh and the spirit and between the kingdom of darkness and the kingdom of light. We Christians are all engaged in this war whether we realize it or not.

Individuals who don't know about God's plan for their lives, on the other hand, are in bondage to evil and have been taken captive by the kingdom of darkness. They are victims of the war but not us. We believers—the people who have been brought out of darkness into God's marvelous light through Jesus Christ—are victors even though we still are engaged in the war. As believers, it is important for us to remember we are destined to prevail! First John 4:4 reminds us, "You are of God, little children, and have overcome them, because He who is in you is greater than he who is in the world."

As I've taught in many nations about spiritual warfare, individuals have responded in ways that show they lack understanding of just what God's Word says about this topic. Some have said, "I'm just not the fighting type," or "Spiritual warfare is not my gift." Others have commented, "I'm not called to that," or "I don't have that type of strong aggressive personality." I've even heard some say, "Now that I'm saved I don't have to fight against the devil." None of their commentary lines up with Scripture.

Furthermore, a Christian might argue, "Jesus has disarmed principalities and powers, so there is no need to fight. We just need to relax and rest in God. After all, the battle is not ours but God's." My response to this argument is it's fallacious. When we accept Jesus into our hearts, we sign up for war. As Paul told Timothy in 1 Timothy 6:12, "Fight the good fight of faith, lay hold on eternal life, to which you were also called and have confessed the good confession in the presence of many witnesses." Later on, Paul told Timothy in 2 Timothy 4:7, "I have fought the good fight, I have finished the race, I have kept the faith." If the above argument was true, Paul wouldn't have spent time telling Timothy this. And if anyone understood what disarming principalities and powers meant, it was Paul. But having that understanding, he writes to us about our engagement in war, encouraging us along with the Corinthian believers that the weapons of our warfare "are mighty through God" (2 Corinthians 10:4). We have to always realize we are in partnership with God in this war, and our victories are won as we are in Christ.

But let's look now at the crux of the aforementioned argument—"the battle belongs to the Lord." This statement appears in 2 Chronicles 20 where King Jehoshaphat is being confronted in battle by the Moabites, Ammonites, and others. When you read the story, you find out that Jehoshaphat didn't just sit at home and rest and allow God to do everything. He and his people gathered to seek the Lord with fasting, and in response to their seeking, the Spirit of the Lord came upon Jahaziel. Then Jahaziel spoke, "'Thus speaks the LORD to you: "Do not be afraid nor dismayed because of this great multitude, for the battle is not yours, but God's. Tomorrow go down against them"'" (15–16). Jehoshaphat and his people had a part to play. The battle of 2 Chronicles 20 was a partnership battle. Martyn Lloyd-Jones helps us understand this by giving us a great analogy.

> The private soldier in the ranks or in trenches during a great battle in a great war is not fighting a private battle; he is not there because he has some personal quarrel. He is just a unit in a great campaign. He does not decide the strategy; he does not even decide the tactics. All that is in other hands. He is in it, he has been called into it, he has been put into his position; but it is not his battle. It is the battle of the King or the Queen or the country, and there is a General commanding and controlling the activities of the army and directing the fight (Lloyd-Jones)

This battle is not a private battle. Jesus is the commander of this army of which you and I are part. I can't emphasize enough that the battle is a partnership battle. God is not going to let you fight alone, nor is He going to fight alone. We are going to fight in partnership.

Yet still other Christians have the notion that spiritual fighting is an exception and not the rule. On the contrary, every day of our lives, we're involved in an emotional, physical, mental, and spiritual fight. We're either going to win or we're going to lose; we'll either be the victors or the victims.

## Our Fight

As we can see by Paul's words to Timothy, the early Church viewed their spiritual experience in terms of warfare. Military terminology is used throughout the New Testament. Protection, for example, is provided for us in the armor of God. The Word of God is compared to a sword. Satan's attacks are called fiery darts. Faith is referred to as the "good fight," and believers are told to "wage the good warfare" (1 Timothy 1:18).

The early Church knew they were engaged in an intense spiritual struggle as should we. Jesus Christ intends the Church to be a victorious army, a united army, an indivisible army, a disciplined army, a combat-ready army poised to stand its ground and not allow the enemy to steal, kill, and destroy the provision and blessing He paid for on the cross. Because of Satan's ongoing attacks, we are called to "endure hardship as a good soldier of Jesus Christ" (2 Timothy 2:3).

Some Christians, however, do not believe the enemy's attacks are ongoing. In fact, I heard someone once say, "Satan will attack you only when you are walking in the will of God." Well, that's true, but that's only halfway true. I'm of the opinion that Satan attacks us in two phases of our lives—when we're walking in the will of God and when we're *not* walking in the will of God. In other words, I believe the devil attacks all the time. That's right. That's his life's goal according to John 10:10. Jesus said, "'The thief does not come except to steal, and to kill, and to destroy.'"

While the war rages, today's Church seems distracted. She's preoccupied with building buildings, producing musical dramas and great worship services, holding fellowship meetings, and fighting brother against brother and sister against sister. It's time for the Church to remember Jesus' words to the multitudes, "'And from the days of John the Baptist until now the kingdom of heaven suffers violence, and the violent take it by force'" (Matthew 11:12).

We must realize our position as the Church of Jesus Christ and not be like the lady who came and said to me, "Pastor, pray for me because Satan is after me." I replied to her, "What is he doing after you? Turn around and go after him!" We should be on the offensive. We should be taking the kingdom of heaven by force. We need to submit to God and resist the devil with the assurance that the devil will flee from us (James 4:7).

## Our Foe's Fear

We ought to remember that even though we are at war with the kingdom of darkness, the devil is afraid of us because we are "the righteousness of God" in Christ (2 Corinthians 5:21). Heaven backs us up. Angels of God back us up. God the Father, the Son, and the Holy Spirit back us up. As far as I'm concerned, the devil panics and dials 9-1-1 (or whatever other emergency number he uses) when he sees a believer who has put on the armor of God and is in the mode of praise and worship to the Father. The devil is afraid of a believer who understands his authority in Christ Jesus. Can't you see that the enemy we are afraid of is actually afraid of us? Remember when God was leading the children of Israel into the Promised Land? The children of Israel were afraid and said that there were giants in the land. In actuality, the people of Canaan were afraid of the Israelites.

Rahab was a harlot in Jericho, a Canaanite city, and she feared for her life and the lives of her family. After hiding the two Israelite spies who had come to view the land, she said: "I know that the LORD has given you the land, that the terror of you has fallen on us, and that all the inhabitants of the land are fainthearted because of you. For we have heard how the LORD dried up the water of the Red Sea for you when you came out of Egypt, and what you did to the two kings of the Amorites who were on the other side of the Jordan, Sihon and Og, whom you utterly destroyed. And as soon as we heard these things, our hearts melted; neither did there remain any more courage in anyone because of you, for the LORD your God, He is God in heaven above and on earth beneath."- Joshua 2:9-11

Another instance in the life of Hezekiah where Hezekiah encourages the people and helps them realize that the enemy is afraid of them. God is at work in their life, for it says in 2 Chronicles 32:78, "'Be strong and courageous; do not be afraid nor dismayed before the king of Assyria, nor before all the multitude that is with him; for there are more with us than with him. With him is an arm of flesh; but with us is the LORD our God, to help us and to fight our battles'" (2 Chronicles 32:7–8).

Hezekiah was also pointing out to the people that although we live in a natural realm, that there is another realm which our physical eyes cannot see. But if God opens our eyes we will realize that those that are with us are more than those against us. He was talking of angels that God has sent to protect and guard. When we look at things in the natural fear will knock on our door, but when we see through the eyes of the spirit at how God is at work, we will realize the enemy has fear of us. We have no reason to fear. Your enemy has every reason to fear, because 'Christ always leads us in triumph [as trophies of Christ's victory] and through us spreads *and* makes evident the fragrance of the knowledge of God everywhere' (2 Corinthians 2:14)

The scriptures also teach that we live in two worlds—the natural world and the spiritual world. The natural world is that which can be seen, felt, touched, heard, or tasted. It is the world of flesh and blood. It's the world in which you and I live and work. But there is another world in which we live. That world is a spiritual world. We cannot see it with our physical eyes, but it is just as real as the natural world in which we live. As a matter of fact, I believe the spiritual world is more real than the natural world because it is the only eternal world.

Paul speaks of this division of natural and spiritual in relationship to bodies. He wrote to the Corinthians about celestial and terrestrial bodies. In 1 Corinthians 15:44, Paul said, "There is a natural body, and there is a spiritual body" (KJV). Every person living on the earth has a natural body made up of flesh, blood, and bones. But we are also spirit beings. We see this more clearly articulated in 1 Thessalonians 5:23, where Paul speaks of man's spirit, soul, and body being presented blameless to God. Our spiritual beings are part of a spiritual world just as our natural bodies are part of the natural world. Within the natural and spiritual realms of which we are speaking, there exist separate kingdoms which are ruled by natural and spiritual leaders.

## Natural Kingdoms

Natural kingdoms are territories ruled by men and women or groups of men and women. Natural kingdoms are countries like the United States, India, China, Kuwait, etc. These are countries that have leaders who may be called presidents, prime ministers, generals, etc. The Bible speaks of these natural kingdoms as "kingdoms of the world." But the problem is that the kingdoms of the world have come under the influential power of Satan. We can see this in the account of Jesus' temptation. Matthew 4:8–9 reads, "Again, the devil took Him [Jesus] up into an exceeding high mountain, and showed Him all the kingdoms of the world and their glory. And he said unto Him, 'All these things will I give You, if You will fall down and worship me.'"

In 1 John 5:19, we see another reminder of Satan's influence. It reads, "We know that we are of God, and the whole world lies under the sway of the wicked one." Although Satan influences the natural kingdom, our God is Lord of heaven and of earth. As the psalmist wrote, "But our God is in heaven; He does whatever He pleases" (Psalm 115:3). He is Lord! God is still the owner of Earth. God is still Lord over the earth. The earth might not accept Him as Lord, but that doesn't change the fact that God is still Lord over all the earth.

## Spiritual Kingdoms

In the spiritual world, we have the Kingdom of God and the kingdom of Satan. Every person alive is a resident of one of these two kingdoms of the spiritual world. The Kingdom of God consists of God the Father, Jesus Christ, the Holy Spirit, spiritual beings called angels, and the saints. The Church is not the Kingdom of God but is part of His kingdom.

The kingdom of Satan consists of Satan, spiritual beings called demons, rulers of darkness, and unregenerate sinners. At the present time in the natural world, the Kingdom of God exists individually within every man, woman, boy, or girl who has made Jesus King of their lives. It exists communally in the true Church and wherever people make this world the kind of world God wants it to be. In the future, there will be an actual visible manifestation of God's Kingdom.

Below, you will see other names used for these two spiritual kingdoms that contrast their differences.

| God's Kingdom | Satan's Kingdom |
|---|---|
| ▪ Kingdom of light | ▪ Kingdom of darkness |
| ▪ Kingdom of holiness and righteousness | ▪ Kingdom of sin and unrighteousness |
| ▪ Kingdom of healing and health | ▪ Kingdom of sickness and disease |
| ▪ Kingdom of truth | ▪ Kingdom of deception |
| ▪ Kingdom of joy and life | ▪ Kingdom of death |

# Living in the Spiritual and in the Natural

As we have discussed thus far, we live in both the spiritual and natural kingdoms. The Apostle Paul points to the order of these kingdoms when he said, "However, the spiritual is not first, but the natural, and afterward the spiritual." God uses natural principles to explain what is happening in the spirit world. That's one reason for Jesus' using parables to teach people about the kingdom of heaven. By using the example of a natural harvest, for instance, He could illustrate the great spiritual harvest to which He was calling laborers. His pointing to something known in the natural helped Him identify for people something unknown in the spiritual.

So, too, when it comes to spiritual war, we can learn a great deal by naturally studying the topic of war. We can understand principles of war that we see in the natural world. These natural principles are applicable to warfare in the spiritual world. In fact, we can say that the nature of this spiritual war is somewhat the same as natural war. The nature of natural warfare is holding onto and protecting land, inheritance, possessions, and people. That is supposed to be the purpose of our military, to protect our borders from invasion and the overthrow of our government by foreign powers. This is the nature of spiritual warfare—hanging onto the territory God has given us through the redemptive work of His Son. We are to keep what Christ paid for on the cross of Calvary. Jesus defeated Satan and bought us the victory. This is clearly pointed out in Colossians 2:13–15, where Paul said:

> And you, being dead in your trespasses and the uncircumcision of your flesh, He has made alive together with Him, having forgiven you all trespasses, having wiped out the handwriting of requirements that was against us, which was contrary to us. And He has taken it out of the way, having nailed it to the cross. Having disarmed principalities and powers, He made a public spectacle of them, triumphing over them in it.

Verses 14 and 15 of *The Amplified New Testament* read, "God disarmed the principalities and powers ranged against us and He made a bold display and public example of them, triumphing over them in Him and in the cross." Additionally, *Weymouth's Translation* of these two verses reads, "And the hostile princes and rulers He stripped off from Himself, and boldly displayed them as His conquests, when, by the cross, He had triumphed over them."

Through Adam, sin entered the human race, and men began to live in defeat, torment, sickness, strife, and failure. But according to these various translations of Colossians 2:13–15, Jesus Christ paid the price for our sins and bought life for us. His investment made on Calvary's cross deposited life, joy, favor, blessing, healing, and abundance into our spiritual bank accounts.

In our natural world, money is a medium of exchange by which we can buy and sell goods. In the spiritual world, the medium of exchange is faith. By faith, we begin to withdraw those things we need from our spiritual bank accounts and make transfers to our natural, physical world. When we begin to do that, we are transformed into the image of Jesus Christ. Our habits begin to change, our actions change, our behaviors change, our attitudes change, and our lifestyles change. The devil hates this, so he puts up a fight. He tries to invade our territory. Our response, then, is to put on the armor of God and fight to keep what rightfully belongs to us.

## Our Defeated Foe

Please understand we are not called to defeat the devil, for he is already defeated. We are at war from the position of victory. We merely are enforcing the victory of the cross. Always remember your authority over the devil because of Christ's victory. You and I are more than conquerors through Him. I'm reminded of an illustration which will help you understand what I've been talking about.

James and his wife were facing great financial difficulties in the early years of their marriage. He worked two jobs, and his wife did all she could, but the finances were not enough to cover the emergencies that had taken place in their lives. One day James saw a newspaper ad of a boxing contest which promised $100,000 to the winner. He looked at the ad and began to think about the possibility of his competing in the contest. He had boxed in his college days and thought it was worth a try. Later, he reluctantly approached his wife about the idea. His wife didn't want him to box again, but since they were in this financial circumstance, she reluctantly agreed.

James began to get up early each morning to exercise and prepare himself to enter the contest. After weeks of training, he entered. After he entered the contest, he began to win every match, and he began to get some money. But the $100,000 was promised to the winner of the final bout. So he thought he'd continue to fight match after match.

Soon, James found himself in the final match. He had made it to the final bout! This was the match where he would either win the $100,000 or go home as second best.

The bell sounded, and the fight began. The first round came and went as did the second, third, fourth, fifth, and sixth rounds. During the seventh round, James finally knocked down his opponent. The whole crowd went wild and cheered. After completing the count, the referee came and lifted James's gloved fist in the air, declaring him the winner—the victor of the fight—and handing him the check for $100,000. James had done it; he had won!

James went home that night to his waiting wife. As soon as he opened the door, she greeted him and asked, "Where's the check?"

James handed her the check. You see, James was the conqueror, but his wife was more than a conqueror! She got the check without having to go one round in the fight. On the cross Jesus once and for all defeated Satan and stripped him of his power. He conquered sin, death, and the devil. Because of Jesus, you and I have been declared, "More than Conquerors." The battle belonged to the Lord, but the victory is yours and mine. Remember you are destined to prevail!

Although the real war has been won by Jesus, you and I must "wage a good warfare" as we continue to hold the territory redeemed for us by our Lord. The pages that follow are my attempt to teach you to how to fight the war that already has been won—how to take back and keep the territory Christ redeemed for you when He defeated death, hell, and the grave. Learn how to live your life destined to prevail!

# Chapter 2

# Paul's Instruction on War

*"Finally, my brethren, be strong in the Lord and in the power of His might. Put on the whole armor of God that you may be able to stand against the wiles of the devil. For we do not wrestle against flesh and blood, but against principalities, against powers, against the rulers of the darkness of this age, against spiritual hosts of wickedness in the heavenly places. Therefore take up the whole armor of God that you may be able to withstand in the evil day, and having done all, to stand "* (Ephesians 6:10–13).

As I've noted before, many people's view on spiritual warfare is distorted. Either they overemphasize spiritual warfare as they see demons everywhere, or they underemphasize it. I've seen those who overemphasize warfare claim everything from their husband's crankiness to their car's not starting the results of demonic activity. To the contrary, those who underemphasize spiritual warfare say things like, "If we don't bother the devil, he won't bother us," or "If we don't study about spiritual warfare, the devil will leave us alone."

In 2 Corinthians 2:11, the Bible says "not to be ignorant of Satan's devices, 'lest Satan should take advantage of us'." At the same time, our thinking should not be consumed with thoughts of demons, for Paul told us "whatever things are true, whatever things are noble, whatever things are just, whatever things are pure, whatever things are lovely, whatever things are of a good report, if there is any virtue and if there is anything praiseworthy—meditate on these things" (Philippians 4:8). So, there's a balance, you see. We need to be balanced in our understanding of spiritual warfare and know that Jesus bought the victory for our lives, but we need to maintain the victory as Satan is constantly trying to take it away. We must, as Scripture admonishes us, "Resist the devil," not "ignore the devil" for that's erroneous. We really need to gain true spiritual understanding regarding this.

Several years ago, I was invited by a local group of believers who have a vision to see our city in revival. They meet quite often to pray and asked me to join in prayer and warfare as they termed it. So I went early morning about 6am on the 42$^{nd}$ floor of a building in our business district. The concept that these believers had was that demon spirits lived in 'high places' and Satan is called the 'prince of the power of the air' (Ephesians 2:2), so believers must find a way to get as high as possible in order to get something accomplished. You can see how somebody could have great zeal and still have some distorted ideas of prayer and warfare. Now if you meet in high places in the city to get a better view of the city and it helps you pray looking over the city then that's great. But the power to pray and exercise the will of God will be no greater on a top of a building or on the ground floor. We need to realize the authority that is placed in our life by Jesus Christ. We need to remove a lot of foolishness which is hindering the life of God flowing through us.

Furthermore, some have the idea that if you are in negative situation then only you will know that you are in warfare. The circumstances of our lives neither prove nor disprove the existence of spiritual warfare. As a matter of fact, spiritual warfare is never absent from our lives, neither should the seemingly absence of trouble or hardship mean we're not in the middle of a fight. You may find this a contradiction of terms, thinking that the absence of conflict means peace. But just as in natural war, there are moments that seem peaceful—where life appears to be continuing as usual with no visible battlefront or fight raging. We know, however, that during times of natural war the enemy is still attacking, having only moved the battlefront to a different location or waiting only for an opportunity to ambush his foes. Regarding spiritual warfare, we must remember we're engaged in the war no matter our circumstances. Our enemy still "walks about like a roaring lion, seeking whom he may devour" (1 Peter 5:8), yet he does not have power over our circumstances. He may be permitted to influence our circumstances, but he does not have charge of them.

Paul's prison epistles, like Philippians and Colossians, affirm this as they assert that the devil is not in charge of our lives. Everything that goes wrong is not from the pit of hell. Every time something goes wrong with your body, with your job, with your family is not necessarily the result of the enemy's attacks. Additionally, not everything that goes wrong in your life is because you are out of the will of God. Many times we are doing things in line with God's Word, and yet we suffer. Paul, for example, was totally in the will of God preaching and teaching, yet the people got hold of him and put him in prison. The good news is that, when you are in the will of God, even a prison becomes a place of opportunity for kingdom expansion.

Acts 28:16 tells us that Paul was permitted to dwell by himself with a soldier. He had a fully dressed Roman soldier in his presence for months. Every day Paul watched this Roman soldier, and each piece of his armor must have been deeply engraved on Paul's mind. When Paul began to pen the Ephesians epistle, the imagery of the Roman soldier was worked out in full detail to illustrate the battle the Christian encounters with evil spiritual powers. So let's heed Paul's instruction on spiritual warfare by carefully studying each part of his admonition in Ephesians 6:10–13. I suggest you read through the book of Ephesians daily as you read this book, allowing the Holy Spirit to bring revelation to you.

## "Finally..."

What does Paul mean by using the term, "Finally"? Is he saying, "I have said everything I wanted to say, so I'm just ending the letter"? Or is he saying, "I'm finishing the letter, and oops, I forgot to mention some more important things"? What does he actually mean? By using this term, I believe Paul is saying this: "All that I have said in chapters 1 through 6 till verse 9 are of utmost importance for understanding and applying what I'm about to say from verse 10 on." That is to say, it's important to understand the basics of what Paul laid out in the previous portions of his text. It's like an athlete who has prepared for months, exercising, lifting weights, keeping a proper diet, and "finally" the day has come for the competition. So in the same manner, Paul uses this term here. All that has been said up to this point gives us a basic foundation for the significant statements he's going to make next.

Watchman Nee, a well-known Chinese Bible scholar, has a great book called *Sit, Walk, and Stand,* dealing with Psalm 1 and Ephesians. In order to understand Paul's "finally" message, I would like to borrow Nee's title. I have always used Nee's three words to tell people the theme of the book of Ephesians. Let's look at the first word, Sit.

## Sit

Sit speaks of our position in Christ Jesus. As Ephesians 2:6 tells us, God has "raised us up together, and made us *sit* together in the heavenly places in Christ Jesus" (emphasis added). Ephesians Chapters 1 through 3 address our position, telling us things like we've been chosen in Him (1:4), adopted as sons (1:5), and sealed in Him (1:13). Furthermore, we read He made us alive "who were dead in trespasses and sins" (2:1) and gave us redemption "through His blood, the forgiveness of sins" (1:7). Also, these chapters address why we have our position, how we obtained it, and why we need to keep it.

The picture Paul paints depicts you and I sitting with Christ, meaning we're reigning with Him like potentates reign in a kingdom. In these specific chapters, Paul shows us our King *sitting* on His throne and shows us *seated with Him.* Our fight, then, in this spiritual war is from a seated position of reigning with Christ—a position of accomplished victory.

Additionally, we know a person sits down when his work is finished. In the same manner, Jesus sat down at the right hand of the Father—"But this Man, after He had offered one sacrifice for sins forever, sat down at the right hand of God, from that time waiting till His enemies are made His footstool" (Hebrews 10:11–12). His work was finished; He had destroyed the works of the devil (1 John 3:8). The work of the cross is finished indeed. You and I are to rest in its finished work. So as Jesus is seated, we are also seated with Him. And as Colossians 3:3 says, we are dead, and our lives are "hidden with Christ in God." When we go into battle, we go in from our heavenly seated position in Christ, not from our earthly position as mere men. Colossians 3:1 encourages us to "...seek those things which are above, where Christ is, *sitting* at the right hand of God."

Our position in Jesus has many benefits. One of those benefits is that our position gives us authority and power on this earth to operate kingdom principles. The dictionary defines authority as the right to command and enforce obedience. Authority grants us the ability to determine justice, issue dictates, and punish violations. A common example of authority is a police officer. What gives a police officer the right to command? It is his position. It is his office. It is his badge that he wears and the authorization that he has received. The badge tells everyone that he is authorized to command and enforce laws in a given jurisdiction. That jurisdiction may be a precinct, a city, a department, a country, or a specific territory. Once the officer steps out of his jurisdiction, his authority and power are no longer recognized, and he can no longer enforce his command. Like the police officer, we as believers are authorized by Jesus Christ to command and enforce the laws of God's kingdom. We have jurisdiction over God's territory because of our position in Christ. Therefore, when the enemy comes against us, there is nothing to fear because we have authority *and power* over him and his works.

Power is one of those words to which the English language does not do justice in communicating biblical truths. In the Scriptures, we find that there are at least five Greek words used for power—*arche*, *exousia, ischus, didomi*, and *dunamis*. Looking at these words, we discover that some of them relate to God and the power He exercises while others relate to man and the power he exercises.

Looking at the first word, *archē*, we find it is used to describe the power of God to create. It is God's power used in Genesis 1:1 to create the heavens and earth. It is the same power God used to create light, and it is the same power that makes us a new person in Jesus Christ. This power is used only by God.

The second word, *exousia*, is translated authority. This authority has been delegated to every person who is in Jesus Christ. Paul boasted about this *exousia* power when he said, "For even if I should boast somewhat more about our *authority*, which the Lord gave us for edification and not for your destruction, I shall not be ashamed" (2 Corinthians 10:8, emphasis added).

The third word, *ischus*, is used to describe prevailing power, penetrating opposition power, and valiant power. This power is in God's Word. We have the privilege to speak it and see results in our daily lives. Acts 19:20 makes this point for us as it reads, "So the word of the Lord grew mightily and *prevailed.*" As does 1 John 2:14b which says, "I have written to you, young men, because you are *strong*, and the word of God abides in you, and you have overcome the wicked one" (emphasis added in both verses).

*Didōmi* is the Greek word used to describe the power to give. It is the power described in John 3:16—"'For God so loved the world that He *gave* His only begotten Son....'" *Didōmi* power enabled the Father God to give His Son. It is the same power that enabled Jesus to give His life as a substitutionary sacrifice for our sins. This power is available to us to live in submission to the laws of Christ.

*Dunamis* is, perhaps, the most recognizable Greek word for power. It is used to describe miracle-working power or the miracle ability of the Holy Spirit. Several New Testament Scriptures speak about this type of power. Jesus said in Acts 1:8, for instance, "'But you shall receive *power* when the Holy Spirit has come upon you....'" In 1 Corinthians 12:10, Paul lists *dunamis* as one of the gifts of the Spirit, "to another *the working of miracles*, to another prophecy, to another discerning of spirits...." Acts 3:7, Acts 4:7, and Acts 19:11 also use this term.

Such power has been given to us by Jesus. The very authority and power He operates in are ours, and we can use them both over the jurisdiction He has given us on this earth. Wow! No wonder the Bible destines us to prevail over the work of the devil—God's given us the power as we are seated with Him! And Paul wanted us to know about our position before he said, "Finally...."

# Walk

The second section of Ephesians, from chapters four to six and verse 9, deals with our walk. This word speaks about possessing the promises of God. To possess means to occupy, to own, to seize, to have it working in your life, to take a hold of, or to control. Ephesians 4:1 directs us regarding our walk — "I, therefore, the prisoner of the Lord, beseech you to walk worthy of the calling with which you were called."

According to Paul, our walk is our personal responsibility. How we steward the deposits God has made in our lives in terms of our gifts, callings, and anointing actually bespeaks our walk. Take Joshua, for example. In Joshua 1:3–9, God told him that every place his foot treads upon belonged to him. Now the opportunity was great. God had promised him and the children of Israel a very vast parcel of land, but it was totally up to Joshua as to how much he was going to walk. If he walked 10 miles, only 10 miles would belong to him. If he walked 100 miles, 100 miles would belong to him. God promised to give a lot of land; as a matter of fact, the boundaries were already set by Him, but it was totally up to Joshua to possess it step by step.

In the same manner, Jesus Christ has disarmed principalities, powers, and rulers of darkness. He has made available the treasures and riches of His grace and glory, but how much we will possess is totally up to us. Of course we don't do the work all alone; the Holy Spirit is in partnership with us in inheriting the promises of God, for He is "the guarantee of our inheritance" (Ephesians 1:13). So walking speaks about possessing the riches available to us — riches of wisdom, spiritual blessing, financial prosperity, vision and purpose, and healing and divine health.

Thus, what we can surmise from the biblical usage of walk is how much we possess of God and our inheritance in Him is totally up to us. We determine how much of the promises of God we will possess. When we decide to walk and begin to possess the promise, the Holy Spirit comes in partnership with us. So Paul encourages us to walk worthy — to walk so as to possess our inheritance in its fullness!

How do we walk so as to possess? Paul teaches us in this epistle to:

- Walk worthy (4:1);
- Walk in humility (4:2);
- Walk in gentleness (4:2);
- Walk in patience (4:2);
- Walk in forbearance (4:2);
- Walk in love (4:2);
- Walk pursuing peace (4:3);
- Walk in unity (4:4);
- Walk not as Gentiles (4:17);
- Walk with a renewed mind (4:23);
- Walk as children of light (5:8);
- Walk circumspectly (5:15).

Herein is another truth Paul wanted us to know and understand before he began to end this epistle in chapter 6. He wanted us to grasp our responsibility to walk worthy, to walk circumspectly, or to walk so as to possess all of our inheritance.

## Stand

The third section, which is Ephesians 6:10–18, deals with our standing. To stand speaks about our partnership in warfare. Unless we know that we *sit* with Christ Jesus in our position of victory and unless we receive grace to *walk* worthy, we will never be able to *stand* firmly. This message of standing is the bull's-eye that Paul is targeting when he says, "Finally…."

With that being said, let's look at what stand means. It means to make a firm decision to hold onto to what you believe and have possessed, and to never let it go. It means that warfare has to do with taking a stand to not tolerate the enemy's attempts to steal, kill, and destroy what God has won for you. You, then, must:
- Stand in covenant with God.
- Stand for your salvation.
- Stand for Jesus in an evil world.
- Stand for your marriage.
- Stand for your faith.
- Stand for your ministry given by Jesus

- Stand for the promises made by Jesus to you.
- Stand for your house.

Second Samuel 23 has a beautiful picture of a person who knows what it means to stand like this. It is an example of the spiritual warfare of standing to which Paul is referring in Ephesians. Verses 11 through 12 read: "And after him was Shammah the son of Agee the Hararite. The Philistines had gathered together into a troop where there was a piece of ground full of lentils. So the people fled from the Philistines. But he stationed himself in the middle of the field, defended it, and killed the Philistines. So the LORD brought about a great victory."

Shammah stationed himself; he took a stand. He stood against his enemies. In the end, after he stood his ground, it was the Lord who brought the victory. Please understand when you decide to take a stand and not tolerate the enemy, God backs you up, and He gives you the victory. You never stand alone; you are always in partnership with Him in this war as you sit, walk, and stand. Now with that knowledge, Paul says, "Finally, my brethren...."

## "My Brethren..."

With this phrase, Paul is emphasizing that He is talking to his brothers and sisters in the family of God. He is not speaking to unbelievers. In the context of his admonition, I do not believe He even is speaking to someone who just has come into the faith. He is speaking to people who have been in the faith and who want to grow up into the things God has for their lives. By using the term, "brethren," I want to suggest to you that Paul is referring to people who desire to mature in their walks.

In the majority of Paul's writing, he seems to make a distinction between saints and faithful brothers and sisters. Saints are those who are in Christ, but Paul's appeals typically reach past the simple saints, preaching a persuasive word to the brethren—the brotherhood whose dedication and commitment move them beyond their comfort zones. Basically, every person who has received Jesus as his Savior is a saint, but Paul goes on to say also that there are those faithful brethren who are really the ones who desire to grow in their

31

walk with God. They continually press into the things of God. I would suggest to you that, by using this term, Paul is saying this teaching is for those faithful ones who desire to grow and who are mature enough to wage war.

## "Be Strong in the Lord and in the Power of His Might..."

Paul tells us here our source of power is God. If we are facing a power outage, it is because we are not connected to the Lord; we're not plugged in properly. Jesus said in John 15:5, "'For without Me you can do nothing.'" Our inability, then, evidences our being "without" Him or disconnected from Him and the "power of His might" or His mighty power.

In the fifteenth chapter of John, we are told to abide in Christ. As long as we live in Christ, we are able to bear much fruit. And as I abide in Christ, I have the same ability that He has. Jesus said in Matthew 28:18 that all authority had been given to Him in heaven and on earth. Later in John 20:21, He also said, "'As the Father has sent Me, I also send you.'" This means that you and I are able to operate in the same power and authority that Jesus was sent with and operated in. Since we are in Him and He dwells in us, we have been empowered by Him and the Holy Spirit to live victoriously—to "be strong in the Lord and in the power of His might."

But Paul is not only telling us who our source of power is, he's adjuring us to be firm, to be steadfast, in God's power. He does this for two reasons. First of all, we must be strong because the devil is powerful. Satan is not more powerful than God, but man cannot face him and win apart from God's strength and enabling. First Peter 5:8 says Satan is seeking people to devour them. Our being strong in the Lord keeps the enemy from doing just that.

Secondly, we must be strong because man without the power of Christ is carnal, sinful, and weak in facing Satan. Over and over in the Scriptures, we see that men and women failed when they walked in their own strength. Without God, they, like us today, had no power to live in victory. We have to persuade ourselves of our weakness apart from Christ. Acknowledging our need and inability apart from Christ is half the battle.

Paul's command to be strong comes from the Greek *endunamoō* which means to empower or enable. Within the Greek text is the inference that Paul's audience has no power except the power God grants to them. That means our power, too, comes only by God's enabling. If God doesn't give you power, then you have no power. The picture that is drawn is *not* of a person who becomes strong by lifting weights, doing push ups, etc. Such people have developed their own strength. The image drawn is of a man being filled with God's power.

In order to become strong in God's power, I would encourage you to sit down and remind yourself of the truth of His power—to consider God's past record. Look at God's power displayed in Genesis 1 at His creation of the world. Look at it in the time of Noah. See His power demonstrated in His parting the Red Sea. See His power exhibited in the wilderness with the children of Israel. Notice His power over the wind and the waves while in the boat with the disciples. Marvel at His power in resurrecting Lazarus. Do you have any doubt regarding His power to enable you to face the enemy?

History has proven time and again that even men and women who walked closely with God doubted His power on occasion. We must combat our own doubt by looking at God's past record in His Word. Specifically, we need to look at the biblical accounts of men and women who doubted God's power. Take Moses, for example, the man who had a face-to-face encounter with God. God called him into the ministry with an audible voice, yet Moses was the very one who said to God, "'The people whom I am among are six hundred thousand men on foot; yet You have said, "I will give them meat, that they may eat for a whole month." Shall flocks and herds be slaughtered for them, to provide enough for them? Or shall all the fish of the sea be gathered together for them, to provide enough for them?'" (Numbers 11:21–22). God reproved Moses with these words, "'Has the LORD's arm been shortened? Now you shall see whether what I say will happen to your or not'" (Numbers 11:23). Miraculously, God sent a wind and brought quail in from the sea enough to feed the Israelites until they were sick of it!

Then, there's Mary whose brother Lazarus had died. She also doubted the power of God. John 11:32 reads, "Then, when Mary came where Jesus was, and saw Him, she fell down at His feet, saying to Him, 'Lord, if You had been here, my brother would not have died.'" Martha also had her doubts. We find this in verse 39 of the same chapter, "Martha, the sister of him who was dead, said to Him, 'Lord, by this time there is a stench, for he has been dead four days.'" Mary limited God's power to the place, for she said, "if You had been *here*," as if Jesus had to be present in order for His power to be exhibited. Martha limited God's power to time by saying, "he has been dead *four days*," as if Jesus was controlled by time. We need to realize that Jesus is not controlled by time nor does He have to appear visibly at the scene, but Jesus can use His power wherever and whenever He wills.

So when in doubt regarding God's power look to the historical evidence in the Scriptures and see how He displayed His power to His people. Remind yourself of the power of God displayed in your own life, too. Use the past to propel you forward. If God has healed you, begin to open your mouth and thank Him by saying, "Lord you have healed me in the past, and you can do it again." Hebrews 10:32 affirms this: "But recall the former days in which, after you were illuminated, you endured a great struggle with sufferings."

Perhaps your struggle is not in doubting God's power but in feeling He's denied you His power. I know I have felt that way before. In fact, we all are tempted by the feeling that God's power has been reserved only for a special few, and we're not of the few. Yet we know Scripture does not teach us this. The truth is, however, He may not be denying us power, rather He may be only delaying our experiencing it. Think of Elijah's being sent to the widow's house only after she had prepared her last meal, or think again of Lazarus who had to experience death before he could experience resurrection life. The widow and Lazarus were powerless until they received His power and until His greater purpose for their lives was fulfilled.

You see, that's another thing we must consider—God's eternal purpose for our lives or, generally speaking, His eternal purpose for man. The first commandment tells us that we are not to have any other gods before Him. Later in Exodus 34:14, we read, "Our God is a jealous God." His eternal purpose, then, is that man trusts Him alone. So when we doubt His power or believe He's denied us His power, we need to remember to consider His record and His eternal purpose for man. As we do this, we then can obey Paul's command to "be strong in the Lord and in the power of his might."

## "Put on the Whole Armor of God..."

"Put on" is a phrase of responsibility. Here we discover Paul's conviction that we are responsible to put on the pieces of armor. Putting on our armor is a deliberate act. When we watch television, for example, we have to make sure we have on our armor. When we are going to school, we have to have it on. When we are going to work, we have to have it on. We can't take it off, as a matter of fact, until we have finished our courses of life. Your armor and your garment of flesh, as it were, will come off together. This means, then, that you and I must walk, work, and sleep in our armor, or we're not true soldiers of Christ. So putting on the armor is a personal choice. We have to choose to put it on and keep it on, for God won't put it on for us, neither will angels nor even our pastors. We are responsible to put on every piece of armor.

Now, let's look specifically at what the Scriptures encourage us to "put on." We must:

- Put on the armor of light—"The night is far spent, the day is at hand. Therefore let us cast off the works of darkness, and let us put on the armor of light" (Romans 13:12).
- Put on Christ—"For as many of you as were baptized into Christ have put on Christ" (Galatians 3:27).
- Put on the new man—"And have put on the new man, who is renewed in knowledge according to the image of Him who created him" (Colossians 3:10).
- Put on the breastplate of faith and love and the helmet of the hope of salvation—"But let us who are of the day be sober, putting on the breastplate of faith and love, and as a helmet the hope of salvation" (1 Thessalonians 5:8).
- Put on tender mercies, kindness, humility, meekness, and longsuffering—"Therefore, as the elect of God, holy and beloved, put on tender mercies, kindness, humility, meekness, longsuffering" (Colossians 3:12).

- Put on love — "But above all these things put on love, which is the bond of perfection" (Colossians 3:14).

God gives us the armor. We are not left to our own resources and devices for our weaponry; no, it's provided for us by Him.. One more thing we need to understand that we don't put on and then take off and then put on. When Paul is saying Put on, he means keep it on. Don't let any kind of laziness, pressures, or temptation get to you to take it off. Once you have put it on, do everything in your power to keep it on.

Twice Paul says, "whole," when talking about this armor we are responsible to put on. He means that we do not pick and choose which parts of the armor we'd like to put on. We have to put it *all* on. By using the term, "whole," Paul is emphasizing that no part of the Christian's armor is to be ignored. Righteousness, faith, salvation, truth, the Word of God, and the gospel of peace must all be worn by the Christian. All of these must cover its respective part on the believer's body. Nothing should be left out. The whole truth of God's Word must be applied to the whole man.

In this spiritual battle we're fighting, you might think, like in the case of natural war, that our armor and weaponry are two different things — the one being used for defense while the other is used for offense. But in spiritual warfare, the armor is also our weaponry. The breastplate of righteousness is not only armor that protects our vital organs, but it's a weapon, too. Proverbs 10:2 tells us that "righteousness delivers from death." Our breastplate, then, can serve as a weapon for our deliverance. Additionally, Jesus said that our knowledge of the truth would set us free. Truth, in this instance, can serve as a weapon bringing about our emancipation. So, our armor serves us defensively and offensively as we face our foe.

I would remind you that we have to make sure that the whole armor is on all the time. Remember what happened to Jacob when he unbuckled his belt of truth and tricked his father for the blessing? He got the blessing all right, but he also was repaid for his action when Laban switched Leah for Rachel. Think how much suffering he might have been spared by keeping on his whole suit of armor. Remember either you destroy the work of Satan in your life by keeping on the whole armor of God or Satan will destroy you. A person who doesn't have the armor on is:

- Alienated from God—"That at that time you were without Christ, being aliens from the commonwealth of Israel and strangers from the covenants of promise, having no hope and without God in the world" (Ephesians 2:12).
- Living in ignorance—"'My people are destroyed for the lack of knowledge'" (Hosea 4:6).
- Impotent—"For when we were still without strength, in due time Christ died for the ungodly" (Romans 5:6).
- Is a friend of sin and Satan—"Adulterers and adulteresses! Do you not know that friendship with the world is enmity with God? Whoever therefore wants to be a friend of the world makes himself an enemy of God" (James 4:4).

One more thing I want to clearly highlight is that the armor that you are getting is a proven armor. Your armor works. It's not test material; it's tested material. It's proven to work, and its provider is God. He guarantees it to work. However, you must put it on—all of it!

## "That You may be able to Stand..."

Why do we put on this armor? Paul answers that question with his pointing to the armor's enabling us to stand. How, then, will we stand? We will stand in covenant. We will stand in perseverance; we will stand because we are more than conquerors. We are going to stand no matter what happens to us—whether we get put into prison or one of our children dies, whether we lose our jobs or everything seems to go wrong. Nothing can cause us to back up, back out, retreat, run away, or fall down because we have geared ourselves up to stand. That's what Paul's admonition here is all about.

When you have made the decision to stand, remember God will not forsake you or allow you to lose strength (Hebrews 13:15). Also, remember Satan cannot pluck a believer out of God's hand (John 10:28). When you have made a decision to stand, God will wrap His grace around you and make sure you are able to do just that.

## "Against the Wiles of the Devil"

"Wiles" is translated from the Greek *methodia*, which means to follow up and investigate by methods, crafty tricks, and schemes. It has the idea of how an investigation bureau would investigate people, plans, and strategies for a case. As you know, such investigations delve deeply into the very personal and intimate affairs of a suspect with investigators leaving no stone unturned.

In the same manner, the devil investigates our lives. He assigns demons to watch us and take notes. He pays attention to how we respond to everyone from our parents to passersby. He notices what irritates us in our relationships. He takes note of the people with whom we have problems. He takes note of how we handle money, people of the opposite sex, and hardship. He pays close attention to our weaknesses, our habits, etc. Understand that you are known in hell. The devil investigates your life and then forms a weapon to attack you — to steal, kill, and destroy the blessings God has given you. But praise God, no weapon formed against you shall prosper (Isaiah 54:17) because you are not ignorant of Satan's devices (2 Corinthians 2:11).

So, pay attention to your walk. Never leave any opening in your life for the enemy to come in. Satan will use every opportunity to enter. He will pound on your emotions. If that doesn't work, he will pound on your relationships. He will pound on your finances. He is always going round looking for an entrance into your life. We have to make sure we guard every door, window, and opening of our lives and live in the righteousness Jesus has provided for us.

## "For we do not Wrestle..."

Paul adds to this by saying we are not wrestling against flesh and blood which we will discuss a little later, but the point is we still wrestle. Paul's use of "wrestle" is quite significant. In Paul's day, wrestling was a popular sport, so Paul used something known in his day in order to provide us with a very useful analogy for spiritual warfare. To wrestle means to contend in struggle for power over an opponent. One important fact you must understand is that Paul is using different words to describe the spiritual war we are in. You might be questioning why Paul would tell us to put on armor to "wrestle" principalities and powers. All he is actually doing here is using different fighting imagery to give us a more accurate picture of the spiritual war in which we are engaged.

Wrestling is not a team sport but primarily a one-on-one contest where one opponent singles out another and enters the arena with him. Such combat is up close and very personal, and its outcome is a true test of an individual's prowess and strength. Armies often fight at some distance; wrestlers only grapple hand-to-hand. You may be able to dodge an arrow shot from a distance, but when the enemy actually has hold of you, you must either resist physically or fall shamefully at his feet.

Our wrestling with the enemy can never be victorious unless we have wrestled with the same Man Jacob wrestled with and lost. Unless and until we have lost to this Man, we can never win over the enemy. Only in complete surrender to Jesus are we able to defeat the enemy.

Let's look now at some facts about wrestling so as to begin to understand more thoroughly just what Paul is trying to say to us about spiritual warfare. First of all, a wrestler requires preparation and training. He must have a proper diet, regular exercise, and know the rules. In the same manner, a soldier of Christ must have a proper diet of God's Word and exercise in prayer on a daily basis. He must know that the enemy will always "fight dirty" while the Christian will have to fight in righteousness. The enemy has no sense of fair play. He has no mercy. He is full of hatred and thrives on torment, but the Christian wrestler always has to fight righteously.

Secondly, in wrestling, a mobile opponent is considered dangerous; that is why you want to pin your opponent down. In the spiritual world, Satan is a mobile opponent. He goes "to and fro" as a lion seeking to devour his prey. You must be on guard for his constant mobility.

Another important strategy in natural wrestling is to upset the balance of the opponent. Once an opponent's balance has been destabilized, he is kept struggling to regain it. The Bible speaks to us of the importance of balance or "temperance." One of the strategies of Satan in the spiritual realm is to try to upset balance. Many cults have resulted because of improper balance on doctrinal issues. Homes, church fellowships, and even nations have been defeated because of imbalance in key theological areas—with certain areas being either overemphasized or underemphasized.

This idea of balance is so important in wrestling. We must understand that there are two types of balance—physical and mental balance. Before physical balance can be destroyed, mental balance must first be undermined. To accomplish this, a strategy of surprise is used. A move is initiated that is distracting and surprising. While the wrestler focuses on this, the intended technique is applied. By leading an opponent to believe some move is about to be attempted, the opponent will try to avoid the imagined danger and leave himself open to the actual attack. How true this is in the spiritual world! Satan upsets balance through the strategy of surprise. He upsets your mental balance by distracting attacks, and while you are fearfully focused on these, he launches his intended assault in another area of your life.

## "Against Flesh and Blood"

You might be thinking that, if our problem is not against flesh, then how come so many times in the Scriptures we find the battle between flesh and spirit? Well, the answer is quite simple. The Scriptures are very clear on the fact that our enemies are three—namely, the flesh, the world, and Satan. By flesh, the Bible means the carnal, sinful nature of man. By world, the Bible means the system of this world which is influenced by Satan. We have to take into account that each of these is a separate opposition we face, and many times each of these is influenced by one or both of the others also. Or put differently, when the Bible narrows down our battle to that of one between flesh and spirit, we must infer the influence these other two enemies have on our flesh.

For clarity's sake, then, I would say our enemies can oppose us in these five different ways:

- Our own flesh can oppose us;
- Our flesh can come under the influence of Satan and oppose us;
- The world can oppose us;
- The world influenced by Satan can oppose us; and
- Satan and his kingdom of darkness can oppose us.

For example, if you are a healthy male, and you see a beautiful lady in a nice dress walking down the street, your flesh may begin to show its ugly face. As Christians, our job is to remind our flesh that it's dead! However, the only thing our flesh knows to do is to respond in a carnal, sinful way. Now that is not caused by Satan. It is simply our flesh which is carnal and sinful by nature. But if we continue to entertain the flesh, it will lead to the devil's influencing that area of our lives.

## "But against Principalities, against Powers, against Rulers of the Darkness of this Age…"

In the kingdom of darkness, there is a great governing and ruling structure. Just as schools, churches, and businesses have authority structures here in our world, the kingdom of Satan has the same; however, his kingdom is made up of principalities, powers, and rulers of darkness.

Additionally, in our natural world, we have several types of forces—the Army, the Air Force, the Navy, and the Marines. These each serve different purposes and functions. The Air Force, for example, does war in the air. It flies planes, drops bombs, and conducts aerial combat. The Navy, on the other hand, does war from the waters, using its ships and shipmen. In the same manner, the kingdom of darkness has different forces that serve in areas assigned by Satan. God, however, has angels and ministering spirits in their assigned places to carry out His plan.

Let's look at four of the different agents of the kingdom of darkness to which Paul is referring.

## Principalities

The root word of principalities is prince, and a principality is a territory over which a prince rules. "Principalities' is taken from the word 'archas' which simply implies 'ancient times'. I believe these are fallen angels who hold the highest position of rank and authority. In fact, principalities are often referred to as territorial spirits. I believe there is a difference between demons and fallen angel. Many people think fallen angels and demons are same to which I disagree.

These fallen angels are placed over a certain region. There are some people who believe that Satan does this geographically. For example, the U.S.A. has 50 states. There are those who believe that there are 50 territorial spirits, controlling their respective state, and each spirit has a different level of control in each state. Now I'm telling you what some people believe not necessarily what the Bible affirms. Looking at some cities or regions, we may see certain sins in preponderance there. For example, prostitution or drugs may be prevalent in one city or region when not in another.

My personal belief is that there are such things as territorial spirits which control certain regions, but I do not believe they control based upon geography; instead, I believe they control based on the prevalence of their being allowed to gain ground in the people living and being there. But Praise God, legally Jesus has disarmed these principalities and given us the right to take over and create an atmosphere of productivity, praise, and purity.

Recently, an evangelist told me every time he visits a particular city he holds evangelistic meetings in the downtown area and some on the outskirts. He was telling me that the downtown meetings are always great. Lots of people get healed, set free from bondages, and accept Jesus as their Lord and Savior. He told me he does not have to do much advertising of his meetings, and people still come by the hundreds. In the same town, moving a little bit out of downtown, he said, it is so difficult. He spends lots of money on advertising and other things to get the people to come in, but the response is not like the downtown area. Even the meetings are not as powerful there. He suggests that because the churches in the downtown area pray and bind the strong man (the "prince" over the area) that there is ease in doing the work of the Gospel. The churches on the outskirts never do anything to gain ground. This may provide us a clue on the importance of binding the strong man over each person, region, family, or church.

## Powers

Powers can be more clearly understood by the word, "authorities." There are many people who have become subject to the enemy's control. These powers or authorities of his kingdom erect strongholds in the lives of people who have continued to walk in evil. Examples of strongholds are evil habits such as drugs, pornography, prostitution, etc. Powers, then, use their evil influence to rule over the lives of people.

## Rulers of Darkness

The Greek word for rulers of darkness is *kosmokratōr*. The same word here in Ephesians is translated, "ruler of the world," in John 12:31. This is a compound word consisting of *kratōs*, which means dominion in the Greek, and *kosmos*, which means the world with its alienation from God. Rulers of darkness, then, simply refer to those demonic spirits that Satan has assigned over governmental structures of this world. These demonic forces concentrate on the leadership or authority figures like the president of a country, pastor of a church, etc. The evil force's main task is to overthrow biblical leadership/authority and replace it with evil, corrupt practices. The rulers of darkness usually try to bring deception through authority figures or governments.

## Spiritual Wickedness in High Places

This simply means domain of darkness in high places. Demon spirit set up a base where they bring in all kinds of vile, vicious, and evil tricks.

Although we are talking about different areas of Satan's kingdom, we need to understand they all work together to get Satan's plan fulfilled. Jesus in Matthew 12 commented about the unity of the devil's kingdom to work together. Another thing to consider is that every prince over an area has a host of demons working. Again in Matthew 12, Jesus gives us insight, by telling us, first the strong man must be bound. Many times, I have noticed that when casting out demons, the demons react and don't want to leave because they are connected to the strong man from which they receive power. So the first thing to do is to bind the strong man over that person, region, etc. When the strong man is bound, the whole host leaves. We will discuss this more in our later chapters. We have to realize that we will see some areas released only when we pray, some when husband and wife pray, some when a family prays, some when a group of believers pray, and some only when a whole church or local churches get together and pray.

It is important to see from the examples of Jesus dealing with demons that he dealt with demons inside of people and demons influencing the person at those moments. We never see any incident that Jesus is fighting against a territorial spirit or any fallen angel. I think it is very important that we deal with the person. I hear many stories of people saying, I'm going to bind principality of a certain region. I think we have to seek God for wisdom in handling situations like this. I believe when you are dealing with a regional thing, it's important that we pray as a church, or by the direction of God get churches together in a city and prayer and worship God. One person cannot go against the principality over a whole region. We need to get the wisdom of God on how to pray and fight in every situation. It's so important to walk by hearing the voice of God.

## "Therefore Take up the Whole Armor of God that You may be able to Withstand in the Evil Day"

Paul repeats the exhortation to put on the armor. In the Pauline writings, we find that whenever Paul saw a truth that was neglected and thought it was of utmost importance he repeated himself. He longed to have the believers forewarned and forearmed. Most of us are spiritually hard-headed at times. We need to have truths hammered home, then, with repeated blows. A preacher should not apologize for preaching the same truth over and over for he can be serving as God's tool to enable us to receive the truth. Paul himself said, "For to me to write the same things to you is not tedious, but for you it is safe" (Philippians 3:1). You should never grow weary of practical truth that helps you progress, that helps you be "safe." So he says again, "Take up the whole armor of God."

The reason we're given to take up this armor is so that we will withstand. To withstand also means to resist. I've mentioned James 4:7 before where James instructs us to resist the devil and he will flee. To withstand or resist means to make a steadfast decision to resist and not just occasionally resist. When the believer continually resists evil, this attitude will become fixed. If you tell a friend not to resist as you push against him, the slightest weight of your hand will cause him to sway. When it comes to resisting the devil, however, mankind has a bad track record. So why don't we resist? We don't resist because we have not yet learned to love righteousness and hate wickedness. If we did, we would stand against and resist him and his schemes.

Paul does not mention specifically what things we should resist, but he says that we have to withstand "in the evil day." What is the evil day? Is it one day? A specific day? According to the Greek, the evil day is a period of undefined length marked by evil in influence and effect. In every generation, there are certain influences of the devil prevalent. What was uncommon in one generation has become the norm in another. In one generation, watching R-rated movies was sin; in another generation, it has become the norm. So Paul is saying in that period of time don't be deceived; keep your armor on.

Times might have changed, but it's the same devil. Proverbs 6:16–19 gives us at least seven things that are an abomination to God and are the very characteristic of this present generation. They are pride, lying, violence, a heart that devises wicked imaginations, feet that are swift in running to mischief, a false witness, and sowing discord. All are prevalent in our present-day world. This is why we need to take up the whole armor so that we can resist the enemy when in the evil day.

## " And Having Done all, to Stand"

What does Paul mean as he closes verse 13? Paul is saying, once you have on the armor, keep it on, stand and use it, and continue to use it to keep standing. Here he implies we will be tempted to get in a relaxed mode. After winning the victory for which we prayed, fasted, and stood in faith, we have a tendency to let our guards down, relax, and then succumb to Satan's assaults. Please understand that many times Satan attacks after the victory. We must never get over-confident. First Corinthians 10:12 tells us, "Let him who thinks he stands take heed lest he fall." Maintain your position in the things of God unlike those in Biblical times who failed after receiving their respective victories. Let's look at some of these Bible examples.

After God established a covenant with Noah, he was found drunk. Abraham, after God made a covenant with him, lied to Abimelech by telling him that Sarah was his sister and not his wife. Moses who saw the power of God work signs, wonders, and miracle failed to enter the Promised Land. These got the victory but failed to keep it by continuing to stand.

But what does it mean to stand? Let me give you several definitions that may help you better understand Paul's last two words in verse 13. To stand means:

- To pull yourself together and brace yourself;
- To be in a position where fear is absent;
- To not go back to the state of comfort or to a place where you felt at ease;
- To maintain proper rank, order, and station; and
- To be alert.

The apostle Paul gives us a great principles that I believe attest to a person who is has chosen to Stand for He writes in Romans 13:11-14, 'And do this, knowing the time, that now it is high time to awake out of sleep; for now our salvation is nearer than when we first believed. The night is far spent, the day is at hand. Therefore let us cast off the works of darkness, and let us put on the armor of light. Let us walk properly, as in the day, not in revelry and drunkenness, not in lewdness and lust, not in strife and envy. But put on the Lord Jesus Christ, and make no provision for the flesh, to fulfill its lusts'. In this text there are 7 characteristics highlighted. Let's look at them briefly.

### 1. Alertness - *"high time to awake out of sleep"* verse 11

This is one of the main characteristics of a person that is to "Stand". Peter in chapter 5 of his first epistle also encourages us to 'be alert'. Remember that Gideon sent back a part of his army because they didn't have the characteristic of 'alertness'. More than ever, we need to be alert to what God is doing, and also the tricks of the enemy.

### 2.   Put off the works of darkness (verse 12)

When we have decided to 'stand' we have to stand in purity before God. We can't allow things in darkness in our relationships, money, our conversation, and our attitude. Darkness is a open door for the enemy to enter.

### 3.   They have the armor of Light

That means our deeds have to be deeds that exhort people to glorify God. That means everything about you should display that you belong to the Kingdom of God.

### 4.   They have a Honest heart

One of the most powerful weapons we have against the enemy is to maintain a pure, transparent heart before God and man. Many come and question our motives? But we have to make sure that our hearts are filled with the plan and purposes of God.

### 5.   There is no dual living (No spirituality mix with carnality)

We learn to love righteousness and hate wickedness. Not many people hate wickedness. They like to mess around on both sides. It's important that we don't even allow the appearance of evil in our lives. (I Thess 5:22)

### 6.   They depend on Jesus not people (verse 14 "Put on Jesus")

When you've decided to stand you are totally leaning on Jesus. **Proverbs 3:5-6** tell us to *"Trust in the LORD with all your heart, And lean not on your own understanding; 6 In all your ways acknowledge Him, And He shall direct your paths."*

People that 'stand' are people who are completely relying on Jesus. They never even for a minute think that it's their strength that will help them stand. This is important, otherwise after the people welcome 'pride' they think that it's their own strength that made them stand.

### 7. Their priorities are on Kingdom Living. (verse 14 "make no provision for the flesh")

People that 'stand' are people that are focused on the Kingdom and not on themselves. When David defeated goliath, he immediately gave praise to God. Any battle that we win is a kingdom victory.

Looking to Paul's words in Romans 13, let us arise from our slumber and take up the armor enabling us to stand in the evil day. Let us press on for the truth. Let us put on Christ so that the light of God can shine in darkness.

# Chapter 3

# How the Conflict Began

### By Pastor Satish Raiborde

*"'How you are fallen from heaven, O Lucifer, son of the morning! How you are cut down to the ground, you who weakened nations!'"* (Isaiah 14:12).

*"Therefore, just as through one man sin entered the world, and death through sin, and thus death spread to all men, because all sinned"* (Romans 5:12).

As I have talked with many people regarding spiritual warfare, I am realizing so many in the Kingdom of God have no clue how the conflict began. They understand by the first man sin came into the world as the above Scripture illustrates. However, many seem to overlook that sin actually began in heaven. It did not begin with a human being but with an archangel named Lucifer, who we now call Satan.

So as we study the Scriptures we must depend on them as the Truth for our lives and submit to the Holy Spirit as He guides us "'into all truth'" (John 16:13). The Holy Spirit is the perfect Teacher, and so let us totally depend upon Him.

As you know, the original Old Testament was written in the Hebrew language while the New Testament was written in Greek.

Very small portions of the New Testament were written in Aramaic, the language that our Lord Jesus spoke. At the outset, let me give you five Hebrew words and their meaning.

*Elohim* is the word for God. It is a plural name; however, when *Elohim* is used, a singular verb is used. This attests to the truth that although He is a triune God, yet He is one. The word, "God" or "*Elohim*," is like the word army or team. There are many people in an army or a team, so in the very same manner in God there is God the Father, God the Son, and God the Holy Spirit—the Trinity in which there is unity.

The Hebrew word for heaven is *shamayim*, another plural word. In English, many times when we desire to make anything plural we add an "s" to a word. In the very same manner in Hebrew, "im" is added.

The term, "*bara*," is used when something is created for the first time. If the same thing is created the second time, this word cannot be used.

The phrase, "*tohu va bohu*," means wasteful or without form or void. It is used to show the cause of judgment.

The fifth word, "*hayah*," is used for the word, "was," but can also be translated as "became."

Many times you might have to refer to these Hebrews words for definition. So now that we've done this let's begin.

Many think that rebellion began when Adam and Eve broke the commandment of God and ate the fruit. But when we look into the Bible, we find rebellion did not begin with Adam but with Lucifer. Lucifer's rebellion is still affecting our world today.

In the beginning, God had created multitudes of angels (the Bible only gives the names of seven of them). It seems from the Scriptures that among these there were three chief angels or arch-angels—namely, Gabriel, Michael, and Lucifer (see Isaiah 14:12, 16; Ezekiel 28:12–18; Daniel 10:10–21; Jude 9; Revelation 12:4). Gabriel means the bringer of good news which attests to what he does. Michael means strong or mighty one. He is also called the prince of Israel. Like his name, he is often involved in warfare. Lucifer means bright or lighted one or shining one. It appears from the Scriptures that each of these archangels may have had one-third of heaven's angels under them.

Study of the Bible gives a clear indication there was another race on this very earth— yes, before Adam (even before the six days of creation in Genesis 1:3–2:1). We belong to the Adamic race. In order to differentiate between the two, we will call the earlier race before the six days of creation as "pre-Adamic" or "pre-Adamite" race. The Bible is a revelation to the Adamic race. What little the Bible tells about pre-Adamic is like a frame to a picture. The picture is the Adamic race while the frame is the pre-Adamics, who were not made in the image of God.

In order to find the root cause of rebellion, it is essential to prove there was indeed the pre-Adamite race on this earth (or shall we call it the pre-Adamite earth). By this, we will know against whom we are fighting and against whom God is fighting. We will address who God's enemies are and how He plans to defeat them.

Genesis 1:1 says, "In the beginning God created the heavens and the earth" (NASB). Now, as we understand God's nature from the Bible, we find that whenever God creates something He always does a "perfect work" (Deuteronomy 32:4). In the beginning, then, God created perfect heavens and a perfect earth. Genesis 1:2 says, "The earth was without form and void." Here the Hebrew word used for 'was' is *hayah* meaning the earth "became without form and void." The Hebrew word for this is *tohu va bohu* which means waste and empty or without form. God did not create it *tohu va bohu*. We learn this in Isaiah 45:18 where a similar expression occurs in the original language. It says, "For thus saith the LORD that created the heavens; God himself that formed the earth and made it; He hath established it, He created it not in vain, He formed it to be inhabited: 'I am the Lord, and there is none else'" (KJV). This verse says, He created it not in vain. He formed it to be inhabited. You see everything that God does, He does with a purpose.

Jeremiah 4:23–26 reads,

I beheld the earth and lo, it was without form, and void; and the heavens, and they had no light. I beheld the mountains, and lo, they trembled, and all the hills moved lightly.

I beheld, and lo, there was no man, and all the birds of the heavens were fled. I beheld, and lo, the fruitful place was a wilderness, and all the cities thereof were broken down at the presence of the Lord, and by His fierce anger (KJV).

We shall make eight observations here. Please open your Bible if you haven't already done so and note the following:

- In verse 23, we find the same phrase used as in Genesis 1:2, "without form and void."
- When was the earth "without form and void"? Was it at the time of Noah? No. The only time it was "without form and void" was before the six days of creation.
- Since the time of Adam, have the heavens ever been without light? At the time of Noah, there was light. There were days and nights. Since the time of Adam, this heaven always had light.
- As we understand the language of the Bible from Genesis to Revelation, the mountains tremble when the judgment of God falls because of sin.
- Verse 25 says, "I beheld and there was no man." When did this happen? Was it at the time of Noah? At that time, eight people were in the ark. Since the time of Adam, was this earth at any time without human beings? No.
- When have all the birds fled? Did this happen at the time of Noah? No.
- When has the fruitful place become a desert?
- When were the cities broken down? And what cities was Isaiah talking about?

From the above observations, we find that the only time the earth was "without form and void" was before the six days of creation. The above account is about the earth before the six days of creation in which there were fruitful places, birds, and people living in cities. The only time when the sun, moon, and the stars of heaven were forbidden to give light on earth was during the period *before* the six days of creation. There had been light on the earth when the earth was created, but then there was darkness until the first day in Genesis 1:3, and since then there has been light every day. I, as do other scholars, believe there was a gap in time between "in the beginning" and when God began to do the work for recreation in Genesis 1:3. The mountains and hills have been moved and will yet be moved by earthquakes. **There never has been a time since Adam to this day nor will there ever be a time from our day unto eternity that the earth has been or will be without a man, bird, or fruitful place.** Jeremiah 4:23–26 cannot be applied to the time of Noah. At that time the heavens had light, there were men, birds, and fruitful places left on earth after the flood.

Scriptures clearly reveal Adam was not the first being on the earth. The earth was created to be inhabited (Isaiah 45:18). It was inhabited from the beginning "by man who lived in cities" (25–26) and by nations (Isaiah 14:12–14). There was a social system on this earth before Adam. These people were mortal and, therefore, capable of being drowned (2 Peter 3:5–8). These beings were replaced by Adam and that's why God gave the commandment to Adam to "replenish" the earth (Genesis 1:28).

Before the six days of creation, we find that water, earth, and darkness were already there. How could this be? From the Scriptures, we come to the conclusion that on this pre-Adamic earth, there were at least three definite things—namely, the Garden of Eden (not the Garden of Eden of Adam), a holy mountain, and a temple.

God appointed Lucifer, who had not fallen at that time, to rule on the pre-Adamite earth. He had at least three offices namely: king, priest, and prophet. As a king he had to rule on the earth on behalf of God. He had one-third of heaven's angels under him to assist him. As a priest, he had to lead the worship to God for the people on earth. As a prophet, he was a mouth-piece for God to the people. One day, pride entered his heart as he Himself wanted to become God—to take His position.

Lucifer spread rebellion among his group of angels with such slanderous suggestions that God had not been fair with them in giving them positions and responsibilities and that they deserved much better. He told them if they would follow him, they would dethrone God and His government. He, then, would set himself up as god and would give them better and higher positions. Lucifer led the revolt from earth to heaven to throw Christ off His throne. But he could never accomplish this.

In Luke 10:18, Jesus says, "'I saw Satan fall like lightning from heaven'" (also see Revelation 12:4). This Lucifer, when fallen, began to deceive the pre-Adamite nation, using slanderous means. God is just, full of mercy and long-suffering. He is a reasonable and very loving God. He gave sufficient time to Lucifer and his angels to repent. But because of Lucifer's stubbornness and pride (which was so great and high that he would not repent but rebelled all the more) God's wrath came on the pre-Adamite earth. We read of this judgment in Jeremiah 4:23–26. God drove him out. Lucifer went on to establish a rival kingdom in the mid-heavens in competition with God (see Ephesians 6:12; Daniel 10:10–21; Ezekiel 28:12–13). God destroyed the pre-Adamic world with a flood. Even science tells you of two floods. Not only that, but also the bones that are found of large animals dating back millions of years are from the pre-Adamic age. This is confirmed in 2 Peter 3:5–7.

> For this they willingly are ignorant of, that by the Word of God the heavens were of old, and the earth standing out of the water and in the water: whereby the world *that then was*, being overflowed with water, perished: but the heavens and the earth, which are now, by the same word are kept in store, reserved unto fire against the day of judgment and perdition of ungodly men (KJV, emphasis added).

"The world that then was" shows us that rebellion did not begin with Adam but with Lucifer.

## The Counterfeit

When God created the angels, He gave them all eternal life without any conditions. God cannot go back on His own Word, and that's why He cannot annihilate or consume Lucifer and his fallen angels. They all have eternal life. There are two kinds of eternal life, however—one with God and the other without Him in the eternal lake of fire, where Lucifer and his angels shall forever be. But it's important to know that every spirit being has eternal life.

Let us look closely at his rebellion against God and his plan for this age. Pride was the first sin of the universe. In Isaiah 14:12–16, please note Lucifer's five "I will's."

How art thou fallen from heaven [fallen from where?] O Lucifer, son of the morning! How art thou cut down to the ground [cut down where?], which didst [past tense used] weaken the nations! For thou hast said in thine heart, *I will* ascend [not descend] into heaven [not out of], *I will* exalt my throne above the stars of God: *I will* sit also upon the mount of congregation, in the sides of the north: *I will* ascend above the heights of the clouds: *I will* be like the most High (KJV, emphasis added).

Do you see what pride and arrogance can do to a person? His "I will" statements resounded from his arrogance.

In Ezekiel 28:12–19, we find more about Lucifer's power, beauty, work, and ways.

Son of man, take up a lamentation upon the king of Tyrus, and say unto him, thus saith the Lord God; thou sealest up the sum, full of wisdom, and perfect in beauty. Thou hast been in Eden the garden of God; every precious stone was thy covering, the sardius, topaz, and the diamond, the beryl, the onyx, and the jasper, the sapphire, the emerald, and carbuncle, and gold: the workmanship of thy tabrets and of thy pipes was prepared in thee in the day that thou wast created. Thou art the anointed cherub that covereth; and I have set thee so: thou wast upon the holy mountain of God; thou hast walked up and down in the midst of the stones of fire. Thou wast perfect in thy ways from the day that thou wast created till iniquity was found in thee. By the multitude of thy merchandise they have filled the midst of thee with violence, and thou hast sinned: therefore I will cast thee as profane out of the mountain of God: and I will destroy thee, O covering cherub, from the midst of the stones of fire. Thine heart was lifted up because of thy beauty, thou has corrupted thy wisdom by reason of thy brightness: I will cast thee to the ground, I will lay thee before kings, that they may behold thee. Thou hast defiled thy sanctuaries by the multitude of thine iniquities, by the iniquity of thy traffic; therefore will I bring forth a fire from the midst of thee, it shall devour thee, and I will bring thee to ashes upon the earth in the sight of all them that behold thee. All they that know thee among the people shall be astonished at thee: thou shall be a terror, and never shalt thou be any more (KJV).

Verses 12 and 13, when read together, are confusing to some people. Verse 12 talks about the "king of Tyrus." Verse 13 says, "thou hast been in Eden, the garden of God." And verse 14 reads, "thou art the anointed cherub." One might ask—what king was in Eden and was an anointed cherub? The earthly king of Tyrus at the time of Ezekiel was Ithobalus II, but this verse is not offered to him but to an *invisible, supernatural* king of Tyre better known as Lucifer. He was in the garden of God in the beginning and had been an anointed cherub. Lucifer rules every nation of this world through his invisible fallen angels. In Ephesians 6:12, this is confirmed. It reads, "For we wrestle not against flesh and blood, but against principalities, against powers, against the rulers of the darkness of this age, against spiritual wickedness in the heavenly places [or in the heavenlies]." When Lucifer fell down, he established a rival kingdom in the mid-heavens, in competition with God.

In 2 Corinthians 12:2, Paul talks about a man who went to the *third heaven.* You see, there can't be a third heaven without a second one, and there can't be a second heaven without a first. Third heaven means the heaven where God Himself dwells. Second heaven means the starry places. First heaven means where the clouds are. It is in the mid-heavens or in the second heavens that Lucifer established a rival kingdom around the earth. The mid-heavens are where Satan has his fallen angels, which rule every nation of this world.

Another instance we read in chapter 10 of Daniel. Daniel had prayed for three weeks. His prayer was heard in the third heavens the same day. But it took three weeks for the answer to come to the earth. Why? Verse 12 says, "Then said he unto me, 'Do not fear,

Daniel, for from the first day that you set your heart to understand, and to humble yourself before your God, your words were heard; and I have come because of your words.'" The same day his prayer was heard, but verse 13 tells the reason for the delay of three weeks— "'But the prince of the kingdom of Persia withstood me twenty-one days; and behold, Michael, one of the chief princes, came to help me, for I had been left alone there with the kings of Persia.'"

Who is the prince of the kingdom of Persia? How can he detain Gabriel, the archangel? Can a man or human being actually detain Gabriel? This verse is not addressing the earthly king of Persia but *the invisible prince of Persia* who is Satan himself, who is the pseudo-god or pseudo-ruler of this world (see Matthew 4:8;, John 8:44;, 2 Corinthians 4:4; John12:31; Ephesians 2:2; 6:10–18; II John 3:8; Revelation 12:7–16; 16:13–16; 20:1–10).

Over every government of every nation of this world, Satan has appointed his trusted fallen angels as rulers to carry out his will and plan in the governments. Each of these rulers is responsible directly to Satan. God also wants to fulfill His own Word of what He Himself has said through prophecy, through His own trusted angels. These, God's angels, carry out His plan and will for governments of the nations as He had predicted, whereas Satan tries to hinder as in the case of Daniel. That is the reason that there is war in the heavenlies between these two groups.

Now, think of Matthew 18:18, where it says, "'Whatever *you bind on earth will be bound in heaven* Now, what can we bind in the third heavens where God lives? Can we bind anything there? This Bible verse is talking about the second heavens where fallen angels try to stop those good angels that come from heaven sent to do the will of God on earth. When you bind fallen angels, then God's angels can come to the earth to act on your behalf.

Why are your prayers delayed so many times? You see, the day you pray, your prayers are heard in the third heaven. When God sends His answers through His angels or ministering spirits, they have to put up a fight in the mid-heavens with the satanic spirits before they can bring the answers to the earth. This is the reason many of the answers to our prayers are delayed. Our prayers and fasting strengthen the angels of God in this warfare and weaken the satanic spirits in the mid-heavens. So we are not ordinary in our faith; we are "heaven shakers." Hallelujah!!!

Fasting is a great weapon, giving special power to weaken and destroy the strength of satanic spirits that try to stop the answers to our prayers. Jesus said regarding the demonized epileptic boy, "'However, this kind does not go out except by prayer and fasting'" (Matthew 17:21). In this kind of warfare, the Church of Christ has to be offensive and not just defensive. We need to remember that:

- All wars lost or won on earth are the results of wars lost or won in the heavenlies between God's angels and Lucifer's angels (see Daniel 13:20–21; 11:1; 12:1; Jude 9; Revelation 12:7–12).

- God seeks to influence, through His angels, every government of this world, and so does the devil through his hosts. Individual lives are influenced daily by good or evil spirits (see Matthew 18:10; 2 Corinthians 10:4–6; Ephesians 6:10–18; Hebrews 1:14).

- Satan was perfect in beauty and full of wisdom until iniquity was found in him. Ezekiel 28:13 speaks of his beauty. Many people think that Satan is a ugly-faced person with 10 heads and hooves. But No! He is still beautiful and can appear as a counterfeit angel of light.

- A loving and long-suffering God gave Satan sufficient time for repentance, but he went on slandering beyond the point of no return because of pride of his beauty and knowledge. So, at last, the wrath of God came upon the pre-Adamite world and the Lord destroyed the earth with a flood.

As we end this chapter, one important conclusion we will deal later on from this study is that demons are not fallen angels and fallen angels are not demons. Demons are spirits of this fallen pre-Adamic race, and therefore they always seek a physical body. Fallen angels, however, have a body of their own kind that is why they cannot possess physical, human bodies. So in the kingdom of Satan, there are fallen angels and demons. We will deal more with this later. It is important to realize this battle is a battle of kingdoms—a battle between Satan and Jesus. Many have sat with me and argued and said, we really don't believe in the pre-adamite world. If you believe the scripture or do not believe, one thing for sure is that when one studies the scriptures, we find that demons are different and fallen angels are different. The purpose of this book is not to give a exhaustive teaching on the subject of pre-adamite world, but to deal with warfare that is delegated to us. So in order for that to happen its important that we understand that demons and fallen angels are in two different categories. The purpose of this chapter was just to help understand that. Maybe you don't agree with what I have submitted before you, but don't stop reading the book, let us keep looking at scriptures for things that will help us in have wisdom and direction when its comes to the war that we face with the kingdom of darkness.

# Chapter 4

# Warfare with the Flesh

—☙

*"I don't understand myself at all, for I really want to do what is right, but I can't. I do what I don't want to—what I hate. I know perfectly well that what I am doing is wrong, and my bad conscience proves that I agree with these laws I am breaking. But I can't help myself, because I'm no longer doing it. It is sin inside me that is stronger than I am that makes me do these evil things. I know I am rotten through and through so far as my old sinful nature is concerned. No matter which way I turn I can't make myself do right. I want to but I can't. When I want to do good, I don't; and when I try not to do wrong, I do it anyway. Now if I am doing what I don't want to, it is plain where the trouble is: sin still has me in its evil grasp"* (Romans 7:15–20, LB).

The Old Testament records many battles and wars that we can look to gain understanding regarding the principles of warfare. However in the New Testament the words 'war' or warfare only occur 6 times. Almost all the references in the New Testament of war or warfare have to do with believers conquering their flesh and walking in the Spirit.

In the church world, prayer seminars have become popular, as have healing and worship seminars. But these meetings don't address the biggest obstacle we have to possessing our victory—our flesh.

When we deal poorly with the flesh, we cannot come into full possession of the promises of God. Many times, I have been in meetings where the people shout at the devil and feel good, but nothing ever is produced for the Kingdom of God because they are not dealing with the sins of the flesh like pride, jealousy, fornication, etc.

When we use the term, "flesh," we are not talking about the physical but the carnal, sinful, fallen nature of man. The Bible also calls the flesh the nature of the old man—the nature meaning the former self who ruled in a person before a born-again experience. This is what's described in Roman 5:12—"Wherefore, as by one man sin entered into the world, and death by sin, and so death passed upon all men, for that all have sinned."

We must never underestimate the terrible power of our fallen nature to hinder and destroy our spiritual lives. Paul tells us in Galatians that the flesh has its lusts or passions. These lusts lead to death. So, Paul admonishes us with these words, "I say then: walk in the Spirit, and you shall not fulfill the lust of the flesh" (Galatians 5:16, KJV).

What is the lust of the flesh? First let us define lust. Lust is strong desire, soulish emotions, the natural tendency of man towards evil. The Bible warns that we should not lust after evil things: "Now these things became our examples, to the intent we should not lust after evil things, as they also lusted" (1 Corinthians 10:6).

Lusting after evil things that will please your fleshly nature is "lust of the flesh." It is how Satan attacks from within. It is like a civil war within a nation except in this case your spirit and flesh war against each other. Our carnal nature, fleshly nature, wars against our spirits because we don't put a guard over our eyes, ears, and thoughts. I have always taught a principle which says, "What you feed will lead." If you feed your spirit, your spirit will lead. If you feed your flesh (carnal nature), your flesh will lead.

How do you feed your spirit? We feed our spirits the Word of God through our eye gate, ear gate, and mouth gate. We need to see the Word (read and study), hear the Word (listen to teaching or reading), and speak the Word (read aloud and use in everyday speech). We need to set our minds and affections on things that are in line with God's Word.

How do you feed your flesh? We feed our flesh by not feeding our spirits and by allowing wrong things to pass through our eyes, ears, and mouths. Watching dirty movies, hearing filthy conversations, and speaking negative things are all food for your carnal nature. Someone has said, I can't stop birds flying over my head, but I can stop them from resting on my head and building a nest. In the same manner, the devil is constantly bombarding us with all kinds of evil, and we have to make sure that we guard our heart, our eyes, our ears, and our mouth. Many times out of ignorance we have allowed the devil to influence our flesh. The Bible says, don't give opening to the devil.

Remember there comes a time where the practice of a particular sin may move from a sin of the flesh (carnal, sinful, fallen nature) to a sin controlled and dictated by satanic, demonic activity. This means that the compulsive inner desire is joined by demonic powers and when this happens a stronghold is developed in your life.

We must be alert and on guard and understand that we are not left powerless. We must heed to Paul's encouragement in II Corinthians 10:4,5 "(**NKJV**) For the weapons of our warfare *are* not carnal but mighty in God for pulling down strongholds,[5] casting down arguments and every high thing that exalts itself against the knowledge of God, bringing every thought into captivity to the obedience of Christ". Here Paul tells us how a stronghold is developed and that we have the power to break and destroy those works of the enemy and not allow it to have a stronghold over our lives. Let's see these progressive stages as Paul has listed them.

Stage 1 – Thoughts

First things first, we must take every thought captive and line it up with the Word of God. If it is left to roam free, it can become a potential threat and a block in the work of God. It is easier to pull a weed out of a garden when it is small, so take those thoughts into captivity in the early stages and don't allow it to become a 'high thing'.

Stage 2 – High Thing

If we allow our thoughts to roam free and don't line it up with the Word of God, it becomes a 'high thing'. It begins to dominate our minds. You constantly begin to think about it. Your free time is really a busy time. Your focus changes. You are consumed with what you are thinking about.

Stage 3 – Arguments

At this stage those thoughts that have become a 'high thing' control you. You tend to defend it. It starts to make sense to you. You have abandoned all insights and tend to be narrow minded.

Stage 4 – Strongholds

Finally, a stronghold has developed. At this stage, it isn't so easy to weed it out.

We have looked at the negative way a thought is developed into a stronghold, but the opposite is also true. We can take thoughts that come from God's Word and allow it to become a 'high thing' and let it dominate our thinking, defend it, and let God's purposes and ways have a stronghold over our lives.

A person, who has allowed the enemy to plant weeds in their life, will bring out works of death and destruction. The Apostle Paul lists the works of flesh when the flesh is not in line with God's Word. Let's look at this and gain some insights.

## The Works of the Flesh

Galatians 5:19–21 presents us the works of the flesh:

Now the works of the flesh are *manifest*, which are these; Adultery, fornication, uncleanness, lasciviousness, idolatry, witchcraft, hatred, variance, emulations, wrath, strife, seditions, heresies, envyings, murders, drunkenness, revellings, and such like: of the which I tell you before, as I have also told you in time past, that they which do such things shall not inherit the Kingdom of God (KJV, emphasis added).

When Paul says, "manifest," he means made known, thus conspicuous before the eyes of men so that all can see for themselves. Paul builds a list of the works of the flesh that falls into five categories:

- Sensuality—adultery, fornication, uncleanness, and lasciviousness;
- Unlawful things in the spiritual realm—idolatry and sorcery;
- Forms of discord—enmities, strife, jealousies, wraths, factions, divisions, parties, and envying;
- Intemperate excesses—drunkenness and reveling; and
- "Such like things"—anything similar in nature to these aforementioned works of the flesh.

## Sensuality

Adultery is the first sensual work of the flesh that Paul mentions. We understand it in our day to mean, as it did in his day, unfaithfulness or voluntary sexual intercourse between a married person and someone other than his/her spouse. Adultery is a specific form of sexual immorality included in the term fornication.

Fornication is the next sensual work of the flesh listed. It refers to sexual immorality in general. It is defined in the lexicons as "prostitution, unchastity, fornication, of every kind of unlawful sexual intercourse," and "properly of illicit sexual intercourse in general."

From the above definitions, a person is guilty of fornication when he/she engages in pre-marital sex (1 Corinthians 7:2–5). The participation in sex by homosexuals and lesbians would fall under the term fornication. Incest also is fornication.

The third sensual work is uncleanness. There are perhaps two ideas expressed in Paul's use of this word:

- One idea is that of physical and material dirt. The word is used to describe the condition that an outgoing tenant is to leave the house free from, that is, free from uncleanness.
- It also indicates moral impurity which is inconsistent with personal purity.

Embraced in the word is whatever is defiling, contaminating, or impure in look, in gesture, in dress, in thought, or in sentiment. When the heathen addressed in Romans 1 became vain in their imaginations, Paul wrote, "Therefore God also gave them up to uncleanness, in the lusts of their hearts, to dishonor their bodies among themselves" (24).

The last word translated, "lasciviousness," is defined as "unbridled lust, excess, licentiousness, lasciviousness, outrageousness, shamelessness, insolence.... lasciviousness: plur. 'wanton (acts or) manners' as filthy words, indecent bodily movements, unchaste handling of male and females, etc." *Webster's New International Dictionary* defines lasciviousness as "lewd, lustful, that which is intending to produce lewd emotions; suiting or proceeding from unlawful sexual desire." This word, then, covers the gamut of sensuality.

## Unlawful Things in the Spiritual Realm

Idolatry is unlawful in God's Kingdom. To help us understand this word, let's first address what an idol is. An idol is defined as "an image, likeness...the image of a heathen god...a false god." W.E. Vine defines idol as "an image to represent a false god...the false god worshipped in an image." Idolatry, then, denotes the worship of deity in a visible form, whether the images to which homage is paid are symbolical representation of the true God (Ex. 20:3–5), or of the false divinities which have been made the objects of worship in his stead.

Idolatry may also be defined as anything that comes between man and God, or better yet, anything that occupies the place in the heart of man that God should occupy. It was for this reason that Paul said that covetousness was idolatry (Ephesians 5:5). Today, few would bow to an image of stone or steel wrought by man's device. But many do practice idolatry by letting other things occupy the place God should occupy in their hearts. Many bow to strong drink, sinful pleasures, drugs, etc. These are inherently wrong and sinful. Fishing poles, golf clubs, boats, camping, etc. are not inherently sinful, but when they come between an individual and his/her service to God, they are as sinful as Baal.

The other unlawful thing in God's Kingdom is sorcery. The original word from which sorcery or witchcraft (KJV) is translated is *pharmakeia*. It is also the word from which our word "pharmacy" is derived. *Pharmakeia*:

> Primarily signified the use of medicine, drugs, spells; then, poisoning; then, sorcery, Gal.5:20.... In sorcery, the use of drugs, whether simple or potent, was generally accompanied by incantations and appeals to occult powers, with the provision of various charms, amulet, etc., professedly designed to keep the applicant or patient from the attention and power of demons, but actually to impress the applicant with the mysterious resources and powers of the sorcerer.

Witchcraft, sorcery, and its related activities may be identified as:

- **Magic**—the use of secret incantations, charms amulets, drugs, special exercises, or other means to tap supernatural beings or non-physical forces to influence someone for another person's benefit. This includes the use of white magic to help or black magic to hurt someone. This does not refer to the typical stage magician who does slight-of-hand tricks.
- **Necromancy**—consultation with the dead for the purpose of receiving information. The supposed occurrence takes various forms. The deceased may appear; the spirit of the dead may appear to possess a living person; the dead may speak through a medium, the sorcerer; or in other ways limited only by the imagination of the sorcerer and the credulity of the seeker. This is spoken of in Leviticus 19:31; 20:6, 27; Deuteronomy 18:11; 1 Samuel 28:7; 1 Chronicles 10:13–14; and Isaiah 8:19. This forbidden practice is useless as a source of information (see also Ecclesiastes 9:1–6).
- **Astrology**—defined by *Webster's New World Dictionary* as "a pseudoscience based on the notion that the positions of the moon, sun, and stars affect human affairs and that one can foretell the future by studying the stars." The astrologer,

then, would be one who seeks information about an individual's decisions, plans, future, and fortunes by charting the stars and planets in connection with his or her moment of birth and life. Not only is this forbidden, it is useless as a source of council (see Deuteronomy 17:2–5; Isaiah 47:12–14; and Jeremiah 10:2).

- **Divining**—the effort to tap some power or spirit so as to discover hidden knowledge, especially to be able to foretell the future or to obtain some special information. Observing times or interpreting omens, portents, and chance events belong under divining. Ezekiel pictures them as consulting images who look into the quiver to discover some hidden knowledge. Sometimes, spirits are called, arrows shot, or special divining rods used (see Leviticus 19:2; Deuteronomy 18:10, 14; 1 Samuel 28:8; 2 Kings 21 :6; Isaiah 2:6; 44:25; Jeremiah 27:9; 29:8–9; Ezekiel 21:21–22; Daniel 2:27; 4:7; 5:7, 11; Hosea 4:12; Micah 5:12; and Acts 16:16).

## Forms of Discord

Enmity is a form of discord. The word translated as enmity has also been translated as hatred, quarrels, quarreling, hostile or hostility, feud, mutual enmity, etc. To hate indicates malicious and unjustifiable feelings toward others, whether toward the innocent or by mutual animosity. In 1 John 3:15, he who hates his brother is called a murderer, for the sin lies in the inward disposition, of which the act is the outward expression. Additionally, James 4:4 includes friendship with the world as enmity with God—"Adulterers and adulteresses! Do you not know that friendship with the world is enmity with God? Whoever therefore would be a friend of the world makes himself an enemy of God."

Another form of discord is strife. The word translated as strife is also translated by the words "variance" (KJV) and "contention." Strife or variance is the expression of hatred or enmity. Whereas enmity is the state or attitude of mind toward other people, strife is the outcome in actual life of that state of mind (see factions).

Jealousy is a form of discord because it "desires to have the same or the same sort of thing for itself." To observe the achievements of another can stir within one the desire to "emulate" or "imitate" with a view to achieving the same worthwhile thing in oneself. This definition may seem harmless, but the flesh can begin to crave something it wants without care or concern of who it hurts or harms to get it.

Wrath is a form of discord that is very violent but very brief. The Greeks said this wrath was like fire in straw, quickly blazing up and just as quickly burning itself out. Wrath, as it is here used, is not long, cherished anger; it is the blaze of temper which flares into violent words and deeds and, just as quickly, dies. Nevertheless, it may result in harm or injury. Paul wrote, "Let all bitterness, wrath, anger, clamor, and evil speaking be put away from you, with all malice" (Ephesians 4:31).

Faction is a form of discord that some Bible versions translate as strife, selfishness, selfish ambitions, intrigues, and rivalry. The *New American Standard Bible* uses the word, "factions," however. W. E. Vine defines this word as "strife, contention in the expression of enmity, Rom. 1:29." Thayer defines it as "contention, strife, wrangling." The word denotes a spirit of personal ambition and rivalry which issues in a partisanship or faction that sets party or personal ambition above service to Christ. Paul exhorted the Romans not to walk "in strife and envy" (Romans 13:13). He even was fearful of returning to Corinth and finding "contentions, jealousies, outbursts of wrath, selfish ambitions, backbitings, whisperings, conceits, tumults" (2 Corinthians 12:20).

Division is a form of discord. It is the opposite of unity which is what Jesus prayed for in John 17:20–21, "'I do not pray for these alone, but also for those who will believe in Me through their word; that they all may be one, as You, Father, are in Me, and I in You; that they may be one in Us.'" Paul, too, pled for unity among the believers, charging "that there be no divisions among" them but that they "be perfectly joined together in the same mind and in the same judgment" (1 Corinthians 1:10). Division does not happen as a result of being led by the Spirit; it is a work of the flesh—"These are sensual persons, who cause divisions, not having the Spirit" (Jude 19).

Other translations translate the word as heresies, party spirit, party quarrels, and factions. W. E. Vine says it "denotes a choosing, choice; then, that which is chosen,

and hence, an opinion, especially a self-willed opinion, which is substituted for submission to the power of truth, and leads to division and the formation of sect. Gal. 5:20." Throughout the book of Acts (5:17; 15:5; 24:5, 14; 26:5; 28:22) the word is translated "sect." The sectarian or denominational view of the church that Jesus bought with His blood is not the Bible view. Every analogy used to reveal some aspect of the church indicates a unity or oneness. The church is viewed as a "fold" and Jesus said there is one fold. It is viewed as a Kingdom in which all who are born again serve King Jesus. It is viewed as a family, the family of God. It is viewed as a body, one body, with each individual being a member. It is pictured as a vineyard with members as workers in that vineyard. Every analogy destroys the contention that the church is to be divided into a multitude of sects, each holding a peculiar doctrine and wearing a different name. The sectarian view is a work of the flesh and not the Spirit.

Envy, another form of discord, has been defined as a feeling of displeasure and ill-will because of another's advantages, honor, possessions, etc. Solomon compared envy in the spiritual realm to something cancer-like in the physical realm when he said, "A sound heart is the life of the body, but envy is rottenness to the bones" (Proverbs 14:30).

Envy has been the cause of some of the most terrible tragedies that ever have occurred. Because of envy, Cain committed the first murder, killing his own brother. (Genesis 4:4–5). The brothers of Joseph sold him into slavery because of their envious heart (Acts 7:9). Saul, Israel's first king, became so envious of David that he hunted him like an animal with evil intentions (1 Samuel 18:8–9).

## Intemperate Excesses

Drunkenness shows excess. Paul said plainly, "And do not be drunk with wine, in which is dissipation; but be filled with the Spirit" (Ephesians 5:18). Peter also addressed that the Christian should not now run to the same riot of excess that formerly characterized his behavior. He said, "For we have spent enough of our past lifetime in doing the will of the Gentiles—when we walked in lewdness, lusts, drunkenness, revelries, drinking parties, and abominable idolatries. In regard to these, they think it strange that you do not run with them in the same flood of dissipation, speaking evil of you" (1 Peter 4:3–4).

Reveling is another form of intemperance. It is used in only two other passages in the New Testament besides our text. It is used in the *American Standard Version* of Romans 13:13, which reads, "Let us walk becomingly, as in the day; not in revelling and drunkenness, not in chambering and wantonness, not in strife and jealousy." It also is employed in the *King James Version* of 1 Peter 4:3, "For the time past in our life may suffice us to have wrought the will of the Gentiles, when we walked in lasciviousness, lusts, excess of wine, revellings, banquetings, and abominable idolatries." *Webster's Collegiate Dictionary* defines the word as, "To be festive in a riotous or noisy manner." Thayer says, "A nocturnal and riotous procession of half-drunken and frolicsome fellows who after supper parade through the streets with torches and music in honor of Bacchus or some other deity, and sing and play before the houses of their male and female friends; hence used generally, of feast and drinking-parties that are protracted till late at night and indulge in revelry."

## Such Like Things

This last category has to do with any additional works of the flesh that are similar to those aforementioned. Paul's admonition to us is to *not* let the flesh have its way. Rather, we are to gain victory over it. He doesn't just warn us, but he gives us three simple keys to overcoming the works of the flesh in Romans 7:15–8:13. He tells us to:

- Understand our vulnerability to walk in the flesh (Romans 7:15–25);
- Crucify the flesh (Romans 8:13); and
- Walk in the Spirit (Romans 8:1–11).

Let us remember Paul's words, "For the law of the Spirit of life in Christ Jesus has made me free from the law of sin and death" (Romans 8:2). You have victory over the flesh. Enforce the principles of God's Word and keep your flesh under discipline. Apostle

Paul says in I Corinthians 9:27 (**AMP**) But [like a boxer] I buffet my body [handle it roughly, discipline it by hardships] and subdue it, for fear that after proclaiming to others the Gospel *and* things pertaining to it, I myself should become unfit [not stand the test, be unapproved and rejected as a counterfeit]. Scriptures will not tell us that we can prevail over the works of the flesh, if it was not possible. So go ahead and Walk in the Spirit for you are destined to prevail.

# Chapter 5

# Warfare with the World

*"Do not love the world or the things in the world. If anyone loves the world, the love of the Father is not in him" (1 John 2:15).*

*"Adulterers and adulteresses! Do you not know that friendship with the world is enmity with God? Whoever therefore wants to be a friend of the world makes himself an enemy of God" (James 4:4).*

The term 'World' has different meanings in Scripture. It can mean the earth or universe in its physical order. It can be used to refer to Gentiles, all nations other than the Jewish nation. But we are using the word here to describe the system that runs the inhabited earth, a system that is opposed to the Kingdom of God.

The world is the whole organized system of social, economic, materialistic, and religious philosophies that have their expression through organizations, personalities, and governments. It is not a specific government, organization, or person, but the worldly system upon which these are based. The world system is an extension of man's carnal, sinful, fallen nature. The reason we are at war against the world, is because the world is run by carnal, sinful people. It provides an atmosphere, an environment, and a system that promote fleshly sins. Here are eight elements in this world of which we need to be aware and mindful:

- **The prince of the world**. As we have discussed already, this world has a prince called, "Satan." So the things of this world are presently influenced by him. They are guided by satanic philosophy and principles. They are flesh-centered and flesh-governed. When Satan came against Jesus in the wilderness, he offered Him the kingdoms of the world if Jesus would worship him (Matthew 3:8–9). Jesus Himself said, however, "'For the ruler of this world is coming, and he has nothing in me'" (John 14:30). Jesus also said, "'Now the ruler of this world will be cast out'" (John 12:31). Remember this ruler or prince won't be in charge too much longer, for one day Jesus will come and take over and set things in order.

- **The structure of the world**. There is great unity in the structure of this world. Even Jesus commented on the unity of its structure in Matthew 12. The world's united structure is in direct opposition to God, His plan, His purposes, and His people. Since this structure is setup by Satan, it is without God. As Ephesians 2:12 tells us, we once were "aliens from the commonwealth of Israel, and strangers from the covenants of promise, having no hope, and without God in the world" (KJV). According to Galatians 1:4, though, Jesus will deliver us "from this present evil world, according to God the Father" (KJV).

- **The spirit of the world**. We in the Kingdom of God are influenced by the Holy Spirit to worship the Father God. Philippians 3:3 verifies this when Paul says we worship God in the Spirit. The spirit of this world, however, demonically influences people to worship Satan. Believers haven't received the spirit of the world, but we have received the "Spirit who is from God, that we might know the things that have been freely given to us by God" (1 Corinthians 2:12).

- **The philosophy of the world**. The world offers knowledge but not based on the Bible. In fact, such knowledge is against the Bible. Its knowledge contradicts God as the creator. That's why Paul warns the Colossians, "Beware lest any man spoil you through philosophy and vain deceit, after the tradition of men, after the rudiments of the world, and not after Christ" (2:8).

- **The wisdom of the world.** This world offers wisdom, but it is totally self-centered. It is not from above "but is earthly, sensual, demonic. For where envy and self-seeking exist, confusion and every evil thing are there" (James 3:15–). Furthermore, 1 Corinthians 3:19 tells us this wisdom is foolishness in the sight of God.

- **The voices of the world.** First Corinthians 14:10 speaks of the world's voices. It reads, "There are, it may be, so many kinds of voices in the world, and none of them is without signification" (KJV). These voices constantly speak the philosophy and wisdom of this world and of its prince.

- **The peace of the world.** The peace the world gives is temporary, fragile, and sometimes deceptive. The peace given by the world is based on human ability and strength. We need the peace that comes through Jesus Christ. "'Peace I leave with you, My peace I give to you; not as the world gives do I give to you. Let not your heart be troubled, neither let it be afraid'" (John 14:27).

- **The attitude of the world.** The world's attitude is that it hates God and His children. Jesus told His disciples in John 15:18–19, "'If the world hates you, you know that it hated Me before it hated you. If you were of the world, the world would love its own. Yet because you are not of the world, but I chose you out of the world, therefore the world hates you.'"

Everyday as you are working out the will of God for your life you can be confident that you live by the faith of the Son of God who lives in you. Your walk might feel like you are marching against a army, but you can be rest assured you are still destined to prevail over the system of this world, and shine as light in the dark as God meant you to be. Let's continue to look at some comparisons between natural warfare and spiritual warfare.

# Chapter 6

# Parallels of Natural and Spiritual War

———❦———

*"However, the spiritual is not first, but the natural, and afterward the spiritual"* (1 Corinthians 15:46).

As we pointed out before, we can gain spiritual insight by looking to natural things. Jesus always used natural things to help His listeners gain spiritual truth. By looking, for example, at a natural, earthly army, we can find spiritual lessons for our fighting this spiritual war. We will take a look at seven features in a natural, earthly army.

## Basic Training

In natural war, no one is allowed to engage in it unless he or she has been trained militarily. Believers, engaged in spiritual warfare, often enter the battlefield without basic training. They may not understand the tactics of the enemy. They may not be aware of their spiritual weapons and how to use them, and they may not have studied the battle plan (God's written Word). David himself testified that warfare has to be learned when he wrote Psalm 144:1—"Blessed be the LORD my Rock, who trains my hands for war, and my fingers for battle." He said in Psalm 18:34, "He teaches my hands to make war, so that my arms can bend a bow of bronze."

In the natural world, to send a soldier to the battlefield without basic training results in defeat. The same is true in the spirit world. When a soldier enters basic training in the natural world, he leaves civilian life behind. He is no longer entangled with civilian affairs but is concerned with the army in which he has enlisted. In the spiritual realm, in order to war a good warfare we must not be entangled in the affairs of life. We are not civilian citizens of this present world. We are warriors of the Kingdom of God. Paul told Timothy, "You therefore must endure hardship as a good soldier of Jesus Christ. No one engaged in warfare entangles himself with the affairs of this life, that he may please Him who enlisted him as a soldier" (2 Timothy 2:3–4)

Martyn Lloyd-Jones on his article on Spiritual Warfare quotes, "A great general once told his troops, 'We are not going to dig foxholes [holes in the ground for hiding] and wait for the enemy to come shooting at us. We are going to move ahead, and move fast. When you dig a foxhole, you dig a grave. When you are in that foxhole and fire at the enemy, he knows your exact location....We will keep moving and the enemy will always hit where we have been and not where we are."

## Surprise Attacks

In natural war there are always surprise attacks. Terrorism, sabotage, and ambush are all surprise attacks and are methods used by natural armies at war. These methods have two things in common: First, they are violent offensive methods. Second, they all have an element of surprise. The target at which such assaults are directed is caught unaware and is unprepared. Confusion and defeat usually result.

Like terrorists who sabotage and ambush, Satan uses the methods of violent, offensive, surprise attacks. He will attack when you least expect it in areas of your life left unguarded. Do not assume the enemy will furnish you with warning of his attacks. This does not happen in the natural world of war; neither will it happen in the spiritual world. The Scriptures admonish us over and over to be alert.

We have to make sure to be discerning, having our hearts pure by God's Word.

## Communication

In a natural war, communication is as important as the weapons the soldier carries. The troops must be able to communicate with their commander to receive instructions and encouragement. The enemy will try to sever communication between the frontline troops and their leader, knowing this will result in failure on the battlefield.

In spiritual warfare, Satan wants to destroy your lines of communication. He will try to prevent you from praying and reading God's Word, as these provide instruction and encouragement for spiritual warfare. If you are so busy at war that you neglect communication with the Commander, you can be easily defeated. Satan always tries to distort our communication. He tries to distort communication between the pastors and his leaders, between congregation and leaders, between husband and wife. There is great power in communication. At the Tower of Babel in Genesis 11, it was the breakage of communication that caused their plans to fail. We always have to be in communication with God, our leaders, and our family. Never, never have a time that you are not communicating, for proper communication will prevent bitterness, unforgiveness, assumptions, hatred, and offenses in our life.

## Targets

In natural war, there are two kinds of targets: moving targets (such as a boat, airplane, tank, or troops) and stationary targets (such as a weapons depository, troop headquarters, watchtowers, etc.). The moving targets are the greatest threat in natural warfare because they are offensive. They are on the move to conquer territory.

In the spiritual world, Satan is most concerned about moving targets. He targets the man and woman who are aggressively moving into the battlefield of spiritual warfare to conquer enemy forces. As I've said earlier, Satan will attack stationary targets also (believers who are not engaged in offensive warfare). The ministry gifts of apostle, prophet, evangelist, teacher, and pastor are ever mobile and advancing. They are a true threat to the enemy as moving targets.

## Mobility

In order to be effective in natural warfare, an army must be mobile. The forces must be able to move to the place where offensive action is to be taken. If they are trapped and held immobile by the enemy, they are ineffective. Mobility is a requirement in the spiritual world if we are to carry out the orders, going into the entire world and preaching the Gospel. Are you a Christian soldier that has been immobilized by the enemy, or are you actively pursuing the command to advance with the Gospel message?

A soldier does not put on armor and take up his weapons just to sit comfortably at home in front of a fire. Remember "A Soldier's Confession" from the first chapter of this book? The soldier not only prepares for battle, he goes to the battlefield. Some Christian soldiers prepare for battle but never leave the security of their homes or church fellowships to go to the battlefield. The war is going on in the streets of our cities. It is going on in villages yet unreached with the Gospel message. No matter how prepared we are spiritually, we will never win the battle unless we are mobile for the Lord Jesus Christ.

Also, a soldier does not gain skills as a warrior by just studying the books on warfare. He advances in skill through experience on the battlefield. Study of your spiritual warfare manual (the Bible) is important, but the battle will never be won unless you put what you have studied into practice. Skill in spiritual warfare comes through experience and application, just as it does in the natural world.

## Team Effort and Obedience

War is a team effort. Soldiers must cooperate with one another and their leaders. They move forward as a united front. They do not fight in their own name but on behalf and in the name of their country. Believers must learn to cooperate in the arena of spiritual warfare. Instead of fighting each other, we need to concentrate our attack against the enemy.

In the natural world when a soldier is wounded, his friends make every effort to rescue him. When the troops move forward, they move as a unit. They do not leave the weak ones behind but place them in the center with strong warriors ahead and behind until the weak ones have recovered from their wounds.

I hate to say it, but the Christian army tends to shoot its own. When a believer falls in battle, we gossip about him or give up on him. Instead, we should rescue these spiritually wounded and surround them with our strength. The forces of God should move ahead as one united front, not as a straggling group trailed by wounded warriors who fall and die by the wayside.

# Dismantling the Enemy's Leadership

In natural warfare, the main leadership is studied. The goal is to dismantle all the leaders one at a time. In the same manner, in spiritual war, we have to understand that the main leadership has already been disarmed, and we need to exercise authority as victors over them. In the kingdom of darkness, the leadership has been stripped off its power, but it still tries to fight. A parallel thought to this is that Satan, along with his demons, tries to target leadership in the family, in the city, in the state, in the country, and also in the church. Always remember to cover your leaders with a shield of prayer. Satan will try to spread rumors about the leadership and try to put a mark on their character, so always be alert. Never allow a direct hit to the leader. As Charles Wesley once said, "Leave no unguarded place, no weakness of soul; every virtue, every grace, and fortify the whole from strength to strength go on, wrestle and fight, stand, pray, tread all the powers of darkness down and win the well-fought day."

# PART II

# Knowing Your Enemy

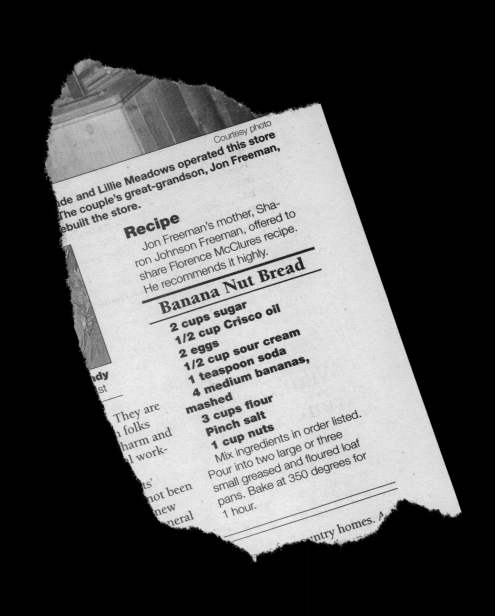

...de and Lillie Meadows operated **this store**. The couple's great-grandson, **Jon Freeman,** ...built the store.

## Recipe

Jon Freeman's mother, Sha-ron Johnson Freeman, offered to share Florence McClures recipe. He recommends it highly.

### Banana Nut Bread

**2 cups sugar**
**1/2 cup Crisco oil**
**2 eggs**
**1/2 cup sour cream**
**1 teaspoon soda**
**4 medium bananas, mashed**
**3 cups flour**
**Pinch salt**
**1 cup nuts**

Mix ingredients in order listed. Pour into two large or three small greased and floured loaf pans. Bake at 350 degrees for 1 hour.

...ndy
...st

They are
...n folks
...harm and
...l work-

...ts'
...not been
...new
...neral

...ntry homes. A

hey g...
...they're cau...
...hake them bad pe...
...? Yes. How are they goin...
...receive help if they aren't pun...
...nack on the hand? If they are or...
...or treatment center while on probati...
...pay for these, and guess what? They...
...ing to pay for the treatment program...
...quick and easy money.
...Drugs are a problem in Lawrence C...
...drug task force will keep kicking in doo...
...still be an influx of meth/drugs in Law...
...unless something is done. It has to star...
...court system.
...If you live in Bedford or surrounding...
...are tired of the drug problem in your co...
...then let the politicians of Lawrence Co...
...how you feel. More than one voice needs t...
...As the late Nancy Reagan said, "Say no to...

## Sending letters

**Letters can** be sent to:
**Mail:** P.O. Box 849, Bedford, IN 47421.
**Fax:** 277-3472.
**Email:** kshetler@tmnews.com.

COMMENTARY

# Ben Fra

he mid...

# Chapter 7

# Common Fiery Darts of Satan

*"Lest Satan should take advantage of us; for we are not ignorant of his devices"* (2 Corinthians 2:11).

*"After all, we don't want to unwittingly give Satan an opening for yet more mischief—we're not oblivious to his sly ways!"* (2 Corinthians 2:11, MSG).

In the first section of this book, we were introduced to spiritual warfare, to how it began, and to battling our flesh and the world. We also were encouraged by the Apostle Paul's instructions concerning warfare and saw parallels between natural and spiritual warfare. Here in this section, we are addressing knowing our enemy. We are living in such times that it is imperative we learn to recognize and know our enemy. Deception has been so common among people because they failed to recognize their enemy.

We must look to God's Word for continued instruction on the character and nature of Satan—our enemy. Scriptures are not silent in speaking out about him. From Genesis to Revelation, we find that many names are used for him. Names often reveal the nature, character, and destiny of a person. The Scriptural names for Satan do just that. Scripture calls him serpent, which speaks of his subtlety and perverted wisdom. The Bible also calls him Beelzebub because he is the prince of demons or the Lord of the flies. Other names are used like tempter, accuser of the brethren, liar, and roaring lion. In our chapter on how the conflict began, we spoke at length about the nature and character of Satan. In this chapter, we want to focus on some of the common strategies he uses. Later on, we will deal with some of the main weapon he uses.

Satan is using specific strategies against Christians to keep the church in a weakened position. Jeremiah 29:11 gives us God's plan for our lives. It says, "'For I know the thoughts that I think toward you, says the LORD, thoughts of peace and not of evil, to give you a future and a hope.'" The opposite of this verse is the devil's plan for your life. The devil's thoughts toward you are to harm you, to confuse you, to put a fear of the future inside of you, to bring disappointment in your life, and to cause you to lose hope. Satan is a killer. He loves to kill. Anything that has to do with death is fully supported and encouraged by him. He is the major influence behind statements like, "I wish I was never born," "I wish I was dead," "The best thing to do is commit suicide," etc.

The Bible warns us not be ignorant of the devices Satan uses, and so it gives us example after example of these devices. His are either fiery darts targeted toward individuals or the Church. Knowing his tactics and schemes will help us be more geared up to face him and thwart his attacks on us and the Church.

## Darts Targeted Towards Individuals

As we talk about the devices used against a believer, remember this: The location where Jesus was crucified was called Golgotha, meaning the place of the skull. If we are to be effective in spiritual warfare, the first field of conflict where we must learn warfare is the battleground of the mind—the place of the skull. An *un*-crucified thought life is an entrance door for the devil. Romans 12:2 tells us to renew our minds. If we stop the work of the devil in the battlefield of the mind, it will never enter into our hearts. Here are some common darts the devil fires at us personally.

## Dart #1: Negative Impression of God

Satan manipulates a believer to create a negative image of God. There are so many that fall having been poisoned by this dart. He'll influence believers to think God is a God of wrath, judgment, and hell rather than love. Satan will blind them to the love of God, causing them to be unfruitful in their walk with God. In the parable of the talents, one individual became unfruitful while the other two saw increase in their investments. The reason for his unproductiveness was that he had a wrong image of his master. He thought he served a harsh master. In the same manner, the devil continually plants seeds of deception like, "Would a loving God allow you to be without a parent?" or "Will a loving God allow your children, wife, or husband to be injured in an accident?" or "Why doesn't God heal you of cancer? Is it because He doesn't love you?"

All of Satan's manipulation begins with things that question God and His Word. Don't fall prey to it. Remember God is a God of love, and His character doesn't change. If Father God was willing to send His own Son to pay the penalty of sin, what more could demonstrate He loves you and has a wonderful plan for your life? Remember Jeremiah 29:11. Go to the Word of God and allow the Holy Spirit to reveal the nature of the Father to you.

## Dart #2: Lies about Approaching God

Many have believed the devil's lies that a certain state of moral excellence must be obtained before coming to God. "You've sinned," Satan says. "Don't go to church. For sure, don't let anybody know," he speaks condemnation to your soul. "If Christians knew what you were really like, they probably wouldn't let you worship with them," continues the accuser of the brethren. "People don't like you because you smoke. They smell the cigarettes on your breath. They know you've been smoking." With such a grievous attack, you begin to think you are not worthy to receive anything from God. If you're not careful, you start to believe his lies about approaching your Father; you'll believe you have to get cleaned up before you can even go to His house.

I would remind you of one of my favorite verses found in John 6:37. Jesus says, "'the one who comes to Me I will by no means cast out.'" Remember we come to the Father so that He can clean us up. We are unable to clean up ourselves. We need the help of Jesus and the Holy Spirit to overcome the things of the world, the devil, and the ungodly desires of our own flesh. God is easy to talk to. God is easy to recognize. He is easy to understand because we have the Holy Spirit as our Teacher. God is easy to approach. Jesus' blood has paved the way for you and I to come boldly into the throne room of God.

## Dart #3: Lies about the Permanence of Change

Satan will tell you change is only temporary. He will tell you that you will never be satisfied in life, that discontentment will always be with you, that you will never completely change. He will say, "You are enjoying God now and going to church, and you think everything is great, but it won't last forever. You'll quit before the end. Look you started so many things in your life, but you could never finish anything, so what makes you think you will change for the good permanently?" Here are more lies from the pit of hell.

The Bible says in Philippians 1:6, "Being confident of this very thing, that He who has begun a good work in you will complete it until the day of Jesus Christ." God is in partnership with you to help you reach your destiny. Confess Philippians 4:13 with your mouth every day, for you can do all things through Christ Jesus who strengthens you!

## Dart #4: Lies about Acceptance

Satan deceives people into thinking they are unloved. The devil says, "You will never be loved or accepted. You're a misfit. You're different. You will never make it in life. Look nobody likes you or cares about you." The reason people believe this lies is because of weaknesses in their lives. He takes their insecurities and magnifies them. Maybe we are different than most people. Maybe we have an accent or are a different color. Remember when lies about acceptance assail you begin to confess with your mouth what is says in Psalm 139:14–16.

I will praise You, for I am fearfully and wonderfully made; marvelous are Your works, and that my soul knows very well. My frame was not hidden from You, when I was made in secret, and skillfully wrought in the lowest parts of the earth. Your eyes saw my substance, being yet unformed. And in Your book they all were written, the days fashioned for me, when as yet there were none of them.

## Dart #5: Lies about Cost

Following Jesus is costly to the carnal nature, but Satan will attempt to scare us about just what the cost might be. Satan suggests you will have to give up certain relationships and endeavors to get you to believe you are going to be lonely, depressed, and lose things or people dear to you. Many of these things are only partial truths. Yes, it costs to follow Jesus, but it costs much more not to follow Him. Yes, you'll have to give up certain habits, relationships, and people, but God will give bless you with other relationships and habits that will bring abundance and satisfaction into your life. Jesus proclaimed, "I have come that they might have life, and that they may have it more abundantly'" (John 10:10). He has given us life more abundantly.

Henry Ward Beecher, a man known for his preaching gift, was in a city campaigning against gambling and drinking. He began to hit these issues so hard that the there was a great stir in the city. One of the businessmen whose business was going down because of Beecher's preaching came to see him with a pistol. He came and pointed it at Henry Beecher and said, "Stop preaching against these things, or I'll shoot you." Henry Beecher said, "Go ahead and shoot. I don't believe you can hit the mark as well as I did." You see, that requires boldness. A man who is following God knows there is no price too high, no cost too great—not even the cost of his own life— that he cannot pay to buy back what Christ purchased for him. The price for not serving and obeying God is too expensive; that price he cannot afford to pay.

## Dart #6: Lies about Self-sufficiency

From the time of Adam and Eve, Satan has tried to encourage man into believing he does not need God. Human reasoning causes a man to think he is capable of being his own god and solving his own problems. Satan says, "Don't waste your time in prayer. Solve problems yourself." But we must not listen to him. We cannot afford to put our own thinking above the Word of God.

One characteristic of disloyalty is elevating your thoughts above God's thoughts as expressed in His Word. There may be times things don't seem to make sense. Something may not seem logical, naturally speaking. The reason for this is that spiritual things have to be spiritually discerned. The truth is some things of the spirit, things of faith, are not so logical. Think of some of the accounts of healing. Dipping in the Jordan didn't make sense, neither did spitting on another man's eyes; both, however, brought healing to men in desperate need of it.

Perhaps, you're sure of your dependence on God. I would remind you of 1 Corinthians 10 where Paul reminded the believers to take heed that they didn't fall. King Asa in 1 Chronicle 14 went to war and won the war against a one-million-people army, but in 1 Chronicle 16 he didn't depend on the Lord and went to man for help. God was very angry and jealous, considering this an act of disloyalty.

James 4:13–16 warns us, "Come now, you who say, 'Today or tomorrow we will go to such and such a city, spend a year there, buy and sell, and make a profit'; whereas you do not know what will happen tomorrow. For what is your life? It is even a vapor that appears for a little time and then vanishes away. Instead you ought to say, '…we shall live and do this or that.'" And Proverbs 16:18 also warns, "Pride goes before destruction, and a haughty spirit before a fall."

# Fiery Darts Targeted towards the Church

## Dart #1: Envy, Strife, and Division

First Corinthians 3:1–3 mentions a triple-headed dart the enemy fires at the Church—"And I, brethren, could not speak to you as to spiritual people but as to carnal, as to babes in Christ. I fed you with milk and not with solid food; for until now you were not able to receive it, and even now you are still not able; for you are still carnal. For where there are *envy, strife, and divisions* among you, are you not carnal and behaving like mere men?" (emphasis added).

ENVY

Envy is defined by *Webster's Dictionary* as "a feeling of antagonism towards someone because of some good which he is enjoying but which one does not have oneself ; a coveting for oneself of the good which someone else is enjoying." <u>According to Vine,</u> "envy is the feeling of displeasure produced by witnessing or hearing of the advantage or prosperity of others; this evil sense always attaches to this word...envy desires to deprive another of what he has." Here are some examples of envy as it is used in Scripture:

- "For where you have envy and selfish ambition, there you find disorder and every evil practice" (James 3:16, NIV).
- "Korah son of Izhar, the son of Kohath, the son of Levi, and certain Reubenites—Dathan and Abiram, sons of Eliab, and On son of Peleth—became insolent and rose up against Moses. With them were 250 Israelite men, well-known community leaders who had been appointed members of the council. They came as a group to oppose Moses and Aaron and said to them, 'You have gone too far! The whole community is holy, every one of them, and the LORD is with them. Why then do you set yourselves above the Lord's assembly?'" (Numbers 16:1–3, NIV).
- "In the camp they grew envious of Moses and of Aaron, who was consecrated to the LORD" (Psalm 106:16, NIV).
- "They have become filled with every kind of wickedness, evil, greed and depravity. They are full of envy, murder, strife, deceit and malice. They are gossips, slanderers, God-haters, insolent, arrogant and boastful; they invent ways of doing evil; they disobey their parents; they are senseless, faithless, heartless, ruthless. Although they know God's righteous decree that those who do such things deserve death, they not only continue to do these very things but also approve of those who practice them" (Romans 1:29–32, NIV).

D. L. Moody told a story about an envious eagle. He saw another eagle flying higher than he could ever hope to fly and immediately was filled with such resentment. Then he spied a hunter. He flew to the hunter and said, "I wish you would bring down that eagle up there."

The man said he would if he had some feathers for his arrow. So the envious eagle pulled one out of his wing. The arrow was shot, but it didn't quite reach the rival bird because he was flying too high. The first eagle pulled out another feather, then another—until he had lost so many that he himself couldn't fly. The archer took advantage of the situation, turned around, and killed the helpless bird.

The best way to get rid of envy is learning to rejoice when others succeed, knowing God is not a respecter of persons. When we honor God and His word, the blessings of His word will come and overtake our lives. We do not have to be envious of people who are being used of God, whose gifting and talents are more public than ours, or who are walking in the blessings of obedience.

STRIFE

Many things may cause strife. For example, we read in Proverbs 10:12 that hatred "stirs up strife." Proverbs 13:10 tells us pride produces strife. Here is a list of other things that produce strife:

- Perverseness—"A perverse man sows strife, and a whisperer separates the best of friends" (Proverbs 16:28).
- Sins of the tongue—"Where there is no wood, the fire goes out; and where there is no talebearer, strife ceases" (Proverbs 26:20).
- Anger—"An angry man stirs up strife, and a furious man abounds in transgression" (Proverbs 29:22).
- Foolish debates and ignorant thoughts—"But avoid foolish and ignorant disputes, knowing that they generate strife" (2 Timothy 2:23).

DIVISION

If there is a common dart of the enemy used against the Church universal, it is the spirit of division. The spirit of division is comes when someone does not understand God's authority and nor respects God's anointing.

In my experience in the pastorate, I have noticed people who are always problematic. They are not only problematic at church but also in their homes and work places. There are many people who cannot submit to a boss in their work place, so they go out and start their own businesses. They become successful and may join a church. But in the church, they cannot get along with people because they cannot tell others what to do; they have to learn to work together. So this causes a problem.

Furthermore, many pastors and leaders in the Church are domineering because they have never learned about authority and submission in practice. With these kinds of attitudes we welcome the spirit of division among us. A person that is able to fully submit to the Lordship of Jesus Christ can also submit to people. The more we allow God to work in our lives, the more we are able to work with one another. **1 Corinthians 12:25 (AMP)** So that there should be no division *or* discord *or* lack of adaptation [of the parts of the body to each other], but the members all alike should have a mutual interest in *and* care for one another

## Dart #3: Toleration of the Jezebel Spirit

Jesus told the church in Thyatira, "'Nevertheless I have a few things against you, because you allow that woman Jezebel, who calls herself a prophetess, to teach and seduce My servants to commit sexual immorality and eat things sacrificed to idols'" (Revelation 2:20). This church came under the influence of a Jezebel spirit.

If you have been a Christian for a while, you have probably heard of Jezebel. Queen Jezebel was the wife of King Ahab. She was the daughter of a Sidonian king who made a trade agreement with Israel's King Ahab. Part of that agreement included Jezebel, the daughter. She was known for the control she exercised and the tactics she used to exert illegitimate and wicked control over people. Her name has become synonymous with the spirit of control.

So a person can be influenced by the Jezebel spirit which controls by the use of manipulative, domineering, and intimidating tactics. It can operate through either gender—male or female—although it is more prevalent in women, but remember it functions just as proficiently through men.

The story of Jezebel is found starting in 1 Kings 17 in association with Elijah. Here we find Jezebel was a very religious person.

Her name meant "without dwelling or habitation," implying her nature was independent and uncommitted. She hated repentance, humility, prophecy, and prayer. Her activity always was characterized by pride, stubbornness, perversion, sexual immorality, and self-centeredness. We will list the features of a Jezebel spirit, but before we do we must understand the spirit of Jezebel is a result of un-crucified flesh. So to remove this kind of monster requires the killing of the flesh and walking in the Spirit.

Here are some of the features of a Jezebel spirit:

- **Critical of leadership**. Just because a person criticize does not mean they have a Jezebel spirit. Here we are talking about people who are very critical and whose criticism is directed towards leadership. Their mouths are consistently given to slander. Usually this is because of secret sins in their lives which they want to keep hidden.

- **Use people to accomplish their own agenda.** These individuals work against the spiritual vision of the church by seeming to be supportive. In actuality, they are against the vision and continually work to destroy it. Sometimes, such people are naïve about the motive behind their own actions; that's how beguiled they can be by the spirit of Jezebel (see Jude 3–4).

- **Independent.** You can never get someone with a Jezebel spirit to submit to work in any area of the church or in relationships. Such an individual is uncommitted. She will always say she cannot commit for some spiritualized reason. In fact, she spiritualizes everything.

- **"Know-it-all" attitude.** Individuals under Jezebel's influence are never reachable, adjustable, or teachable. They are always busy doing something more important than what the church is doing, and they also have a negative attitude towards the church's teachings and activity. Although they know it all, it's amazing they still want to be a part of the church.

- **Mock the prophetic.** They ridicule whenever some prophesies by pointing to others some of the character traits or history of that person prophesying to invalidate the prophecy.

- **Refuse to admit wrongdoing.** A man influenced by Jezebel will never admit he's wrong, unless it is a temporary admittance of guilt to gain "favor" with someone. He will always show how much he's done and never get to the point where he acknowledges how much others have done for him.
- **Receive correction as rejection.** Whenever these individuals receive correction, they always end up crying and acting as if they have been rejected. I believe this is an endeavor to receive more attention by claiming they've been wronged instead of acknowledging they've done any wrong. Often, they will accuse others of having rejected their spiritual gift, claiming we would not receive it or them.
- **Pushy.** When in need, a woman influenced by the spirit of Jezebel wants compassion. However, she is never compassionate towards others who are in need. She will demand for herself what it is she wants and push until she receives it.
- **Sow seeds of discord.** Sowing discord is very diabolical in that a man under Jezebel's influence will seem to sound an alarm, alerting others to an assault of the enemy while he himself is part of the assault. Yet he will attempt to look innocent because, after all, he alerted everyone else to the problem at hand. Sowing seeds of discord may also involve such a man's calling people and telling them past events and histories of people, situations, etc. Whenever someone seems to enjoy pulling things from the past that are negative, it is always associated with the devil. Jesus closed our past by the seal of His blood.
- **Always talk intimidation.** They are always talking in terms of what is legal and illegal, using the law as a means to maneuver people and situations. They always create a sense of fear whenever they give input in anything. They use fear and intimidation as leverage to suit their own purposes.

These are simply guidelines that are found in the scripture just because someone you know is a little controlling doesn't mean they have a Jezebel spirit. I think all of us in one way or another are a bit controlling. We have to see and hear the direction of the Holy Spirit in dealing with situation and not just look at natural circumstances.

When the enemy has launch an all out attack against the church we don't need to panic, but understand that when a flood is coming, the Holy Spirit is the first one on the scene. . **Isaiah 59:19 (AMP) tells us that** 'When the enemy shall come in like a flood, the Spirit of the Lord will lift up a standard against him *and* put him to flight [for He will come like a rushing stream which the breath of the Lord drives].' We are not ignorant of the devices of the enemy. We will stand tall and not allow the work of the enemy to penetrate in our lives. You are destined to prevail.

# Chapter 8

# Satan's Army

*"For they are spirits of demons, performing signs, which go out to the kings of the earth and of the whole world, to gather them to the battle of that great day of God Almighty"* (Revelation 16:14).

Satan's army consists of fallen angels and demons. Most of them have different ranks, and levels of authority, and that's the reason Paul in Ephesians mentioned we fight against principalities, powers, rulers of darkness, and wicked spirits.

In our chapter on how the conflict began, we talked a little bit about fallen angels. Here, however, we will address demon spirits. The Scriptures often use the terms, "devils" or "spirits." There is only one devil while there are numerous demon spirits (evil spirits) of like nature and character.

When we study the ministry of Jesus, we find that Jesus on a regular basis dealt with demons. Although the Old Testament on many occasions notes the presence and activity of demons, we never find any ministry of a person expelling demons until Jesus. The Scriptures disclose some people who tried to expel demons but not by the authority of Jesus. Their attempts were through some evil practices.

The expelling of demons was the most striking feature of the ministry of Jesus compared to any person used of God before His time. There are historical records of the resurrection of the dead, of miracles of healing, and of multiplication of food, but only the New Testament has records of the expelling of demons.

It is most amazing to observe the ministry of deliverance in the life of Jesus. Most of the time, we would think He was expelling demons from people who were not believers. Most of the people Jesus delivered, however, were religious Jews. These were believers of the Law and of the traditional history passed down from their forefathers. So many times I have seen people who are born again, filled with the Holy Spirit, and speaking in tongues in need of deliverance because they have opened a certain area of their lives to the control of the devil. These are the people we assume are free, but they have allowed bitterness, unforgiveness, hatred, etc. to give the enemy a foothold.

As we look to the Scriptures in regards to the work of Satan through demons, remember that Jesus never commissioned anyone in the Scriptures to go and preach the Gospel without commissioning them to cast out (expel) demons. It's important to know your enemy. In dealing with demons, we must understand some important things about them. Let's make some observations about them.

## Demons are Real Personalities

Demons possess both will and intelligence and act according to their evil natures (Matthew 8:29–31; James 2:29). Demons have the ability to speak, and of course they speak when they are in a human body. Demons also have emotions for it says in James 2:19, "You believe there is one God. You do well. Even the demons believe— and tremble!"

Many times, in the ministry of Jesus, demons spoke and told their names, even at one time saying how many of them were present. There is no place in the Bible that endorses any lengthy conversations with the demons, though. I believe it is wrong to have any lengthy conversation with demons because it will lead to other demonic practices or will open a door you don't want to open.

Demons cannot stand hearing the name of Jesus or speaking about the blood of Jesus. Many times, when I went to visit people at their house, the members of the household who were possessed knew I was coming and had left before I got there. Demons cannot stand even the presence of righteousness.

## Demons are Spirit Beings

Although demons are spirit beings, they have no body. This explains the reason for their seeking to possess the body of humans. (Matthew 8:16; Luke 10:17, 20; Matthew 17:18).

## Demons are Satan's Servants

Demons are enslaved to Satan by choice (Matthew 12:22–30). One point to observe is that demons will always acknowledge Jesus as the Holy One, Anointed, etc. They will never acknowledge Him as Lord. Satan will never permit them to call Jesus, "Lord." We don't find any case of this in the Scripture. For one reason, Satan wants the demons to call him Lord. Please understand this is only an observation from what's recorded in the Scripture; it is not a fact.

## Demons Enter the Human Body

Because demons are looking for a dwelling place, they may enter the human body, and several can be present in one body at once. On one occasion, a demon admitted to Jesus that his name was Legion, "'for we are many'" (Mark 5:9; Luke 8:2, 30). We find many occasions in the Scripture where Jesus expelled numerous demons at one time from a single person. Although demons prefer human bodies, they will enter into animals also.

In expelling demons, I have observed they will always try to make the situation comedic and not serious. They do this by making funning faces, funny voices, and poking fun at the elements of Christian belief. I have heard and seen people who need deliverance sing songs and dance to non-Christian songs and call Satan as king, ruler, leader, guru, hero, etc. Always control the situation by speaking the Word of God and the name of Jesus to maintain order.

## Demons are Symbolized

Satan and his hosts are symbolized through the Scriptures, providing us with clues to his strategy. Each symbol reveals his nature of operation. Below is a list of some of the symbols. These symbols may be idols that individuals possess in their houses, around their necks in a form of a chain, around their hands, etc. We need to remove any of these symbols and idols or anything that gives the expression of the work of Satan.

- Fowl of the air (Matthew 13:4,19);
- Unclean birds in a cage (Rev 18:1–3);
- Unclean Frogs (Rev 16:13–14);
- Locusts from the bottomless pit (Rev 9:1–10); and
- Serpents and vipers (Luke 3:7).

In Christendom, we have various symbols like the ark of God, the cross, the dove, etc. On the same note, we see symbols of the devil in some forms of dolls (ugly dolls), serpents, strange crosses, etc. Keep in mind, there is no power in these symbols or idols, but they may be a point of contact in which the evil work is released. If the woman with an issue of blood could touch Jesus and get healed, the same principle applies negatively. Of course we know that it was the woman's faith and the garment was only the point of contact. I have known people in our meetings who have come for deliverance, and when we are praying for them and command demons spirits to come out, many of them tell us how they got in. We have people who have testified that they kept posters of movie and rock stars and used to look at them everyday and did their hair like them, tried to talk like them, wore clothes like them, etc. This was a point of contact. They literally began to idolize the people on posters.

## Demons Manifested in Different Ways

When Jesus exposed demons they fell down and cried (Mark 3:11), they frothed at the mouth and physically abused their victims (Mark 9:20, 26–27), and they caused their victims to look as if they were dead after their removal (Mark 9:26). When I have expelled demons in the name of Jesus, I have seen people vomit uncontrollably, scream in pain, make foul expressions, and also make hands and feet turn in angles that they normally could not turn. I have also experienced a foul smell that was unbearable. I have walked into people's homes or into areas in a city where there is a foul smell, something you cannot detect naturally, unless the Spirit of God activates your discernment. Also many times, I have smelled a certain odor connected with certain sinful practices.

## Demons can Control Sickness in a Person's Body

There are many instances in the Scriptures that as soon as evil spirits or demons were expelled their victims were healed immediately. In Luke 13:11, the woman who had been plagued for 18 years with the spirit of infirmity was bent over and could not straighten herself up. Jesus told her, "'Woman, you are loosed from your infirmity'" (Luke 13:12). He laid His hands on her, "and immediately she was made straight" (Luke 13:13).

With the demonized mute boy, Jesus said, "'Deaf and dumb spirit, I command you, come out of him and enter him no more!'" (Mark 9:25). "Then the spirit cried out, convulsed him greatly, and came out of him. And he became as one dead, so that many said, 'He is dead.' But Jesus took him by the hand and lifted him up, and he arose" (Mark 9:26–27).

When I started going around preaching the Gospel, I began to see a lot of people getting healed and coming back after few months for healing of another type of sickness. Some people got healed three or four times with different sicknesses, each after another. I wondered why, and then I realized often a sickness is controlled by a spirit. You have to rebuke and cast out the spirit, and then the sickness will go also. If the person is healed, and the spirit is not cast out, it will manifest in other sicknesses. As believers, we have to learn not only to receive our miracle and healing but to maintain it, enlarge it, and multiply it.

## Demons have Different Levels of Wickedness

Jesus pointed to demons having different levels of wickedness when speaking about the individual who has been delivered. He said the unclean spirit will go looking for a place where it can rest. When it cannot find such a place, Jesus continued, "'Then he goes and takes with him seven other spirits more wicked than himself, and they enter and dwell there; and the last state of that man is worse than the first. So shall it also be with this wicked generation'" (Matthew 12:45).

I submit to you that demons fight for a higher level of wickedness among themselves. They constantly want to reach a next level in their duties. They crave worship. They are proud of their wickedness and their drive for moving deeper in darkness. I have seen people voice that they are proud to do wicked things even to believe that is their destiny. Any person who is proud of his wickedness definitely is in need of deliverance, and this is very hard to do, unless the person submits to the conviction of the Holy Spirit. Only the Holy Spirit can melt this type of pride.

## The Names of Demons Bespeak Their Purpose

The Bible gives names of several evil spirits. Here are some of them:

- Spirit of fear—"For God has not given us a <u>spirit of fear</u>, but of power and of love and of a sound mind" (2 Timothy 1:7).
- Spirit of error—"We are of God. He who knows God hears us; he who is not of God does not hear us. By this we know the spirit of truth and the <u>spirit of error</u>" (1 John 4:6).
- Spirit of jealousy—"'"If the <u>spirit of jealousy</u> comes upon him and he becomes jealous…"'" (Numbers 5:14).
- Spirit of prostitution/adultery/fornication—"'They do not direct their deeds toward turning to their God, for <u>the spirit of harlotry</u> is in their midst, and they do not know the LORD'" (Hosea 5:4).
- Spirit of heaviness/depression/despair/discouragement—"'To give them beauty for ashes, the oil of joy for mourning, the garment of praise for the spirit of heaviness…'" (Isaiah 61:3).
- Spirit of perverseness/sexual addictions/uncleanness—"'I will also cause the prophets and the unclean spirit to depart from the land'" (Zechariah 13:2).
- Spirit of sickness, disease, and infirmity—"And behold, there was a woman who had a spirit of infirmity eighteen

years, and was bent over and could in no way raise herself up" (Luke 13:11).

## Demons Oppose God's Ministers

Demons do not want the Gospel to be preached. They will oppose God's ministers, thereby hindering the preaching of the Gospel. Jesus addressed this in part when He spoke the parables of the different soils. He said, "'When anyone hears the word of the kingdom, and does not understand it, then the wicked one comes and snatches away what was sown in his heart. This is he who received seed by the wayside'" (Matthew 13:19). The Apostle Paul, too, attested to demons who oppose the ministry of the Gospel when he wrote to the Thessalonians, "Therefore we wanted to come to you—even I, Paul, time and again—but Satan hindered us" (1 Thessalonians 1:18).

## Demons Blind the Minds of the Unbelievers

Paul spoke of those who are perishing, who are unbelievers, in 2 Corinthians 4:4. He said of them, "whose minds the god of this age has blinded, who do not believe, lest the light of the gospel of the glory of Christ, who is the image of God, should shine on them." This is what demons do—they blind the minds of men.

## Demons Seduce People

To seduce means to imposter, mislead, lead astray, allure, or tempt. The Apostle Paul warned Timothy about those who would depart from the faith. He said in 1 Timothy 4:1 that they would depart because they had listened to seducing or deceiving spirits.

## Demons Torment and Vex People

To vex means to molest, harass, or bring pain. Scripture clearly indicates demons do just that. Acts 5:16 reads, "Also a multitude gathered from the surrounding cities to Jerusalem, bringing sick people and those who were tormented by unclean spirits, and they were all healed."

## Demons Enslave People

Demons enslave people with certain habits. These habits become addictions or compulsive behaviors. We have people who have habits like overeating, immoral sexual habits, alcoholism, cigarette addiction, etc. When we consistently give in to these activities that may be driven by demons, we become very compulsive in our behavior. I have seen people hurt their own families through physical harm, abusive words, and stealing money, never giving it a second thought. They'll even say they don't know why they do what they do.

## Demons have a Doctrine

Today, we have countless examples of men and women who have compromised the truth and have not endured sound doctrine. Paul consistently reminded Timothy to hold fast to sound doctrine, "Now the Spirit expressly says that in latter times some will depart from the faith, giving heed to deceiving spirits and *doctrines of demons*, speaking lies in hypocrisy, having their own conscience seared with a hot iron, forbidding to marry, and commanding to abstain from foods which God created to be received with thanksgiving by those who believe and know the truth" (1 Timothy 4:1–3, emphasis added). According to this Scripture, demons have a doctrine. In fact, it forbids marrying. Doesn't that sound familiar? I have heard people say that they don't have to get married; they don't need to have "the paper" as proof of their love. Well according to Paul, that's a demonic doctrine they're subscribing to.

Its important to realize that as we are studying the scriptures to gain understanding of our opposition that we don't loose sight of the authority we have been given by Jesus Christ to stand as victors in every circumstance. Greater is He that is living in you and me than he that is in the World. Jesus is Lord.

# Chapter 9

# Can a Christian be Demon-possessed?

*"'Be angry, and do not sin'; do not let the sun go down on your wrath, nor give place to the devil"* (Ephesians 4:26–27).

The topic of this chapter is a hot one! Divisions and breakdowns in relationships have occurred because of how many have chosen to answer this question. In no way am I trying to prove that I'm right about what I set forth here, but I simply want to point out some Scripture and some of my own experience.

Let me first say I believe the English language has generated the heat for this debate. In English, for example, a man can say, "I love pizza," and "I love my wife." Both statements employ and apply the same word for the man's pizza and his wife, yet we would hope the man feels a little more passion, care, and concern for the love of his life. In many Eastern languages, on the other hand, there are different words to accurately describe your feelings for a person, a place, or things. As far as the debate at hand is concerned, evil spirit, unclean spirit, and the devil are all used interchangeably in the English language. When, for example, we find people who have demonic influence we may say he or she has a devil. Actually, what we mean is that person is under demonic influence. We must remember there is only ONE devil and MANY demons.

Another word we've used in the English language when speaking about those under demonic influence is "possessed." The problem with the use of this word is that it suggests ownership and not influence. So when you say a person is possessed by demons, it is suggesting that person is owned by the devil.

Let me say very clearly that I do not believe a person who is born-again and filled with the Holy Spirit can be owned by the devil. I do believe, however, a person who is born-again and filled with the Holy Spirit can allow certain parts of his or her life to be under the influence of demons. Now let me balance it by saying, if a born again, filled in the Holy Spirit person continues to allow the influence of the devil to lead him, he can become totally owned by the devil. In such a case, he is no longer a Christian that is possessed; he is simply a person that is owned by the devil. Jesus is no longer the Lord of his life, but the Devil is.

Demons can only influence believers to the extent we allow them to do so. That's why Paul says in Ephesians 4:27, "Don't give any place to the devil." I have seen many people give place to the devil in their lives and never repent. They keep living in the same sin, and so the devil took more ground in their life, and soon, they were at a place where they were fully owned by him, doing his bidding. They had abandoned the Lord Jesus Christ as their Savior and chose the god of this world. Believers that are usually under the influence of demons have pretty much toyed with sin and have never rid themselves of the sin. These people typically fall prey to demonic influence through the following:

- Illicit sexual practices (pornography, addiction to X-rated movies);
- Deep-seated anger, bitterness, unforgiveness, rage, heavy metal music, rejection, alcohol, drugs, etc.;
- Attraction to the occult; and
- Generational sin or curses (when not dealt with).

Satan's domain or rule of authority is darkness, and Jesus' domain is light. Wherever there is darkness, Satan needs no permission to enter and carry out his plan. Luke 11:35 warns us by telling us to watch out that the light within us does not become darkness. But how can the light in us become darkness? Simple, when we harbor sin and don't repent or when we have pride, lust, lies, vain imaginations, etc., we are creating a domain of darkness; we are giving place to Satan because these are fruits of darkness. That's why we even have believers who are oppressed by the devil and demons.

Oppression means a person is weighed down with something that she is not able to carry or is not designed to carry. So whenever there is darkness, it is an open door for Satan to oppress you. We find in the Scriptures that many are oppressed through disease, through fear, through discouragement, through criticisms. When we don't take care of these areas by using the authority that Jesus gave us, we go deeper into the problem—moving from oppression to obsession.

Obsession means a person has given some areas of his life to an evil spirit which is preoccupied persistently with an idea or emotion that usually has no relationship with reality. Many men are obsessed with pornography. Their eyes are filled with lust and are unable to see anything pure and holy. Some of these men are living dual lives, serving Christ yet giving themselves over to the lust of their flesh. When this is not dealt with, they begin to give more and more areas to the devil—to the point that the man becomes possessed or owned by the devil. Then he has no will power over his life; the devil controls him. It is only through the power of the Holy Spirit and the Word of God that people can live in freedom.

Here is my final suggestion on this matter. Instead of spending time finding out if a Christian can be possessed, let's spend time in the presence of God, whereby we are made and kept pure via His Holy Spirit. Then, we'll flee every appearance of evil, and we won't allow even the smallest area of our lives become a place for the devil to discredit us.

# Chapter 10

# Seeking Deliverance from Demons

—

*"Therefore submit to God. Resist the devil and he will flee from you. Draw near to God and He will draw near to you. Cleanse your hands, you sinners; and purify your hearts, you double-minded"* (James 4:7–8).

As we've been studying the Scriptures, maybe you are realizing something in your own life that you need to address. Maybe you know someone else who has come under this influence of demons and are losing the war. I want you to know that the Word of God has the answer and solution for us to set things in order and walk victoriously. Remember there is always victory in Jesus, and you are destined to prevail!

We want to look to Jesus as our great model in this warfare. He overcame the world, the flesh, and the devil. We are to be imitators of Him. Here are a few simple steps to take for deliverance.

## Recognize

The apostle John wrote, "In this the children of God and the children of the devil are manifest: whoever does not practice righteousness is not of God, nor is he who does not love his brother"

(1 John 3:10). We must recognize that we cannot be practicing unrighteousness and saying we are of God. In areas where we recognize we're not practicing righteousness, we must be willing to submit those areas to God as James 4:7 admonishes us. The first step is to recognize that we've fallen prey to the work of demons. Then, we must have a desire for deliverance. Well how can you be sure you're struggling with the demonic? Simply ask yourself, "Do I have a continuous desire to practice righteousness or unrighteousness?"

Many people recognize they're bound but don't really have a desire to be set free. Some choose not to be free because of deception. The demons have told the person, "If you ask this person to pray for you, we will come with a lot more demons to trouble you, or we will kill you." Deception and fear are controlling them. Remember, before we can rebuke and resist the devil, we have to submit ourselves to the authority of God. Secondly, we have to be willing to receive deliverance. Remember the freedom is paid for by the work on the cross by Jesus Christ. Your freedom is God's mercy made available to you.

In the Book of Mark chapter 5 we see seven signs that help us recognize the influence of demons.

1. Isolation ('had his dwelling among tombs' – verse 2-3)
2. Loss of Self control –('no one could tame him' verse 4)
3. Nakedness (Mark 5:15)
4. Separation from Family (Mark 5:3)
5. Self-Destructive ('...crying out and cutting himself' verse 5)
6. Emotional Torment (Mark 5:5)
7. Mental Illness (Mark 5:15)

## Rebuke & Repent

It is very important that you verbally rebuke and bind the demons in the name of Jesus. Jesus asked the Pharisees, "'How can one enter a strong man's house and plunder his goods, unless he first binds the strong man?'" (Matthew 12:29). By His example, also, Jesus taught us to rebuke the demons. He rebuked the unclean spirit in the man that was in the synagogue. That is why it is important to rebuke and bind the demons. Your tongue filled with the power of God's Word is a great weapon to renounce, resist, quench, and annihilate the work and plans of Satan.

Renouncing the works of the devil and repentance go hand in hand. Repentance means to make a complete turn-around in your walk. It's like the story of the adulterous woman caught in the act. Jesus told her to go and sin no more. As Paul told the Corinthians, "But we have renounced the hidden things of shame, not walking in craftiness…" (2 Corinthians 4:2). You should renounce those things, and once you have been delivered, don't practice the same things that opened the doors for the demons to enter. If need be, get some strong believers to come and pray with you and help you in this process.

## Reclaim & Replace

We need to reclaim every area that has been damaged by demonic influences. Again, your tongue is the key to reclaiming and replacing. The name of Jesus is the authority by which we are able to do this. So use your tongue and command in the name of Jesus that every area that has been affected to be reclaimed and brought in line with God's Word, God's purpose, and God's direction. We need to reclaim those areas and begin to replace it with what God's Word says about them. We need to reclaim and replace our position in Jesus Christ. We need to reclaim and replace our posture of victory. We need to reclaim and replace our ability to love.

If your relationships have been damaged because of demonic influences then you have the right to speak God Word and begin to reclaim and replace the things that have been damaged. For example, you could pray that God will help you build stronger, godly relationship that will enhance your walk with God. I have a friend who had been tormented by demons for over 10 years. In the process he was very unstable emotionally, and his family thought he was mentally ill. He could not even read or write. After he was delivered he began to reclaim and replace those areas affected and claim God's word. He began to confess everyday that he has the mind of Christ. After some time, God began to restore his mind and he became brilliant in his thinking and went to college and got a Phd. No one had any hope that this man would even been able to read or write. Praise God. If the devil affects any area of your life, God is out to reclaim, replace, and restore on a higher level.

## Renew

After you have reclaimed and replaced every area the enemy has affect make sure to continually renew. You have to renew your minds. Renew your strength. Renew your thoughts. In Matthew 12 when Jesus spoke about demonic spirits leaving its dwelling, looking to find rest elsewhere. If you'll recall, the Bible says that when the unclean spirit left, the house was swept and put in order but still empty. Remember your eyes, your ears, and your mouth are gateways for blessing or cursing. So focus your eyes, ears, and mouth on the purposes of God, and you will find yourself refilled and renewed on a daily basis.

# PART III

# The Believer's Armor

# Chapter 11

# The Belt of Truth

*"Stand therefore, having girded your waist with truth..."*
(Ephesians 6:14).

To put on the armor of Christ is not to put on an unscriptural fanaticism or to use a louder voice in prayer. To put on the armor of God simply means to put on CHRIST. And every piece of the armor is a virtue or characteristic of Christ Himself. Spiritual warfare can only be won if we mature in Christ, learning how to stay dressed for battle. Spiritual warfare is not praying loudly, listening to or employing a certain type of music, or screaming the name of Jesus. Real Spiritual warfare is putting on Christ. To put on Christ is to put off the works of the flesh.

As we discussed in an earlier chapter, there are six pieces of armor the Apostle Paul instructs the Ephesian church to put on. When we study the Roman Soldier as per the history book we find that they had more armor and also weapon than what Paul has listed. Paul never meant this to be exhaustive. Other aspects to warfare are also valid, but he picks out the most important and helps us apply them. The order in which the armor pieces are labeled, I think, is of importance. I don't think Paul listed these pieces of armor haphazardly as they might occur to him. I believe he was building a case. I believe he was establishing a pattern.

The belt was the first piece to be put on. It was central to all the armor. The soldier kept his money, his sword, his writing instrument there. The belt kept the breastplate in place and gave the soldier firmness in his dress. It was not mere decoration or adornment. We have to remember that Paul was writing for his own day and generation when it was custom for people, men included, to wear long and loose garments. The belt was used to tuck in the garment. A solider would never leave his garments blowing in the wind. Otherwise, he would constantly step on them or stumble on them when handling the sword. So the first thing the solider always did when he was getting ready to meet the enemy was to gather all his clothing together and fix it firmly in position by using the belt or girdle. This made him ready. He was alert, and he was set for action.

The Apostle Paul connects truth with the Belt. Belt material is truth—truth as opposed to falsehood, truth as opposed to hypocrisy, truth as opposed to fantasy. What is Paul's meaning of truth in this context? I've heard people claim truth means nothing more than a spirit of sincerity and honesty. They relate this to David's saying, "You desire truth in the inward parts." They say this because they believe this "belt of truth" does not mean the Word of God, for the Sword of the Spirit is the Word of God. To me in studying the Scriptures, this seems like a dangerous interpretation. If we are going to rely upon our sincerity and truthfulness as a piece of armor in the fight with the devil, then we are already defeated. Are you prepared to trust yourself? Paul reminds us that the armor is provided by God; therefore, it is not part of ourselves but something that we are able to put on, as it is given by God. As far as my understanding goes, it is impossible to be honest, truthful, and sincere without the Word of God applied in my life through the power of the Holy Spirit. Man left to himself is deceitful. The book of Jeremiah declares that the heart is deceitful above all else.

So, what is Paul's meaning of truth in this context? I believe the belt of truth is also the Word of God; it's simply being used in a different manner. Let me explain. When Jesus was fasting and praying in the wilderness, Satan tempted him thrice. Each time Jesus answered by declaring "It is written". There Jesus was using the Word of God as the sword of the Spirit. Jesus was quoting a particular Scripture which is very different from talking about the *whole truth* of the Bible. Therefore, I believe the belt of truth is the *whole truth* of the Word of God, while the sword of the Spirit is *a particular truth,* or I would even go as far as saying, prophetic or present truth of the Scriptures. Jesus did not quote all of the statutes, commandments, testimonies, and judgments of God's Word, but he quoted particular, specific truth.

Another way to help us distinguish between the belt of truth and the sword of the Spirit is to refer to the belt as *the written, living Word of God* and the sword of the Spirit as *the quickened Word of God.* Quickened means made alive and applicable to a particular situation by the Holy Spirit. The belt of truth is all of Scripture from Genesis to Revelation while the sword is a particular, specific Scripture applicable and made fitting by the Holy Spirit.

To help us see this, we need to look at the two words used to describe the Word of God in Greek—*Logos* and *Rhema. Logos* means the living, written Word of God—the Holy Scriptures. *Rhema,* on the other hand, is the quickened Word of God. Rhema refers to a specific statement; it is the illumination of specific parts of the *Logos*—specific statements from the general knowledge. That is why I said above that the belt refers to the Logos—written, living Word of God, and the sword of the Spirit refers the quickened Word of God or *Rhema. Rhema* will come when *Logos* is known.

So the belt of truth—the *Logos*—is the first thing Paul mentions. So the first thing we need to learn to do is to deposit the Word of God in our lives. Without it, we are completely lost. Without, it the breastplate won't fit. Without it, there is no place to put the sword of the Spirit. Without it, all the garments are loosely moving, thus creating a hindrance. And as Ephesians 4 says, we need the truth in our lives so that we are not "tossed to and fro and carried about with every wind of doctrine" (14).

The belt of truth, then, is put on as we abide in God's Word. Jesus said to those Jews who believed Him, "'If you abide in My word, you are My disciples indeed. And you shall know the truth, and the truth shall make you free'" (John 8:31–32).

*So* how do we abide in God's Word so that the belt of truth is put on? To abide in God's word is accomplished by our studying and meditating on God's Word. The Apostle Paul told Timothy, "Study to shew thyself approved unto God, a workman that needeth not to be ashamed, rightly dividing the word of truth" (2 Timothy 2:18, KJV). And as the Lord told Joshua, "'This Book of the Law shall not depart from your mouth, but you shall meditate in it day and night, that you may observe to do according to all that is written in it. For then you will make your way prosperous, and then you have good success'" (Joshua 1:8).

So, if the belt of truth, is the *Logos* of God's Word, then it becomes the responsibility of every believer to deposit the *Logos* into his life. Many have the idea that we only study if we are doing the work of the ministry like being an apostle, prophet, pastor, evangelist, teacher, missionary, etc. Please understand the devil doesn't care whether you are a prophet or a teacher in a school or if you're a businessman, for that matter. He is out to steal, skill, and destroy, and you better put on the belt of truth by reading, studying, and meditating on the *Logos* of God.

A man without the Word of God (*Logos*) is likened to many things in the Scriptures. A man without the Word of God is like a:

- Man in the darkness without a lighted lamp (Psalm 119:105);
- Ship without a rudder—just drifting;
- Boat without a sail—driven by any and every wind;
- Ship without a helm—directionless;
- Person without a compass—lost, not knowing his whereabouts;
- A house without foundation—unstable;
- A plant without sun—lifeless; and
- A man without a map—no sense of direction.

There is tremendous power in God's Word. God's Word does the following for us.

- Gives life—"'It is the Spirit who gives life; the flesh profits nothing. The words that I speak to you are spirit, and they are life'" (John 6:63).
- Produces faith—"So then faith comes by hearing, and hearing by the word of God" (Romans 10:17).

- Brings healing—"My son, give attention to my words; incline your ear to my sayings. Do not let them depart from your eyes; keep them in the midst of your heart; for they are life to those who find them, and health to all their flesh" (Proverbs 4:20–22).

- Nourishes our spirit, soul, and body—"Therefore, laying aside all malice, all deceit, hypocrisy, envy, and all evil speaking, as newborn babes, desire the pure milk of the word, that you may grow thereby..." (1 Peter 2:1–2).

- Gives new birth—"Having been born again, not of corruptible seed but incorruptible, through the word of God which lives and abides forever" (1 Peter 1:23).

- Produces light—"The entrance of Your words gives light; it gives understanding to the simple" (Psalm 119:130).

- Produces wisdom—"Get wisdom! Get understanding! Do not forget, nor turn away from the words of my mouth. Do not forsake her, and she will preserve you; love her, and she will keep you. Wisdom is the principal thing; therefore get wisdom. And in all your getting, get understanding" (Proverbs 4:5–7).

- Gives victory—"Your word I have hidden in my heart, that I might not sin against You" (Psalm 119:11).

- Gives cleansing—"'You are already clean because of the word which I have spoken to you'" (John 15:3).

- Releases and produces worship of the Father God—"'God is Spirit, and those who worship Him must worship in spirit and truth'" (John 4:24).

- Produces joy—"'These things I have spoken to you, that My joy may remain in you, and that your joy may be full'" (John 15:11).

- Produces hope—"And take not the word of truth utterly out of my mouth, for I have hoped in Your ordinances" (Psalm 119:43).

- Makes you offense-proof—"Great peace have they which love thy law: and nothing shall offend them" (Psalm 119:165, KJV).

- Makes you fruitful and prosperous—""If you walk in My statutes and keep My commandments, and perform them, then I will give you rain in its season, the land shall yield its produce, and the trees of the field shall yield their fruit"" (Leviticus 26:3–4).
- Releases favor with God and man—"Let not mercy and truth forsake you; bind them around your neck, write them on the tablet of your heart, and so find favor and high esteem in the sight of God and man" (Proverbs 3:3–4).

As we have looked at the importance of first putting on the belt of truth in our life, take a honest look at your life and see if any areas of your life are beginning to fall apart. If you are loosing peace in a certain area of your life, or if you are feeling condemned, and anything of that sort and mostly assuredly you realize that you have been loosening the belt of truth or not making a priority in your life to put it on. So let's make it a habit and a priority to put on the belt of truth and embrace our position as winners.

# Chapter 12

# The Breastplate of Righteousness

*"Stand therefore, having girded your waist with truth, having put on the breastplate of righteousness"* (Ephesians 6:14).
*"But to do this, you will need the strong belt of truth and the breastplate of God's approval"* (Ephesians 6:14, LB).

*"'No weapon formed against you shall prosper, and every tongue which rises against you in judgment you shall condemn. This is the heritage of the servants of the* LORD, *and their righteousness is from Me,' says the* LORD*"* (Isaiah 54:17).

The enemy desires to destroy every believer who desires to put on the armor for warfare. He desires to destroy our inner strength by damaging our consciences, confusing our emotions, corrupting our desires and affections; therefore, we must put on the breastplate to protect our will, and affections.

Righteousness simply means right-standing. It means that you are in right-standing with God. Righteousness is the absence of the guilt of sin, the accusation of sin, and the condemnation of sin. In Biblical language the words, "righteous" and "justified," come from the same root word. Justified means made righteous or just. This means a believer in Christ is not guilty for his sin when tried in the courts of heaven. You see, the Bible says in Romans 5:17, "For if by the one man's offense death reigned through the one, much more those who receive abundance of grace and of the gift of righteousness will reign in life through the One, Jesus Christ."

In this verse, we notice two heads of creation—namely, Adam, the head of the old creation, and Jesus, the Head of the new creation. Adam's one offense brought about condemnation, guilt, sin, and death. Jesus' one righteous act of obedience brought about grace and a life of righteousness. In Adam, sin was reigning. In Jesus Christ, grace reigns. In Adam, man was a slave of death. In Jesus Christ, man is a slave of the grace of God. On the cross, Jesus became our substitute for the penalty of sin. He died for us as our substitute, and we died with Him in identification. The Bible says we:

- Were crucified with Him (Romans 6:6);
- Died with Him (Romans 6:3, 8);
- Were buried with Him (Romans 6:4);
- Are planted together with Him (Romans 6:5);
- Are raised with Him (Romans 6:9);
- Are seated together with Him in victory (Ephesians 2); and
- Are alive with Him (Romans 6:8).

This, then, is what we know:

- When Christ was crucified, the believer was crucified.
- When Christ died, the believer died.
- When Christ was buried, the believer was buried.
- When Christ arose, the believer arose.
- When Christ ascended, the believer ascended.
- When Christ sat down with all things being under His feet, the believer also sat down in the throne, and all things are under the believer's feet.
- When Christ lives, and as He lives, so the believer lives.

In understanding the above, we come to the conclusion that the supreme court of heaven has imputed the righteousness of Jesus to man. As 2 Corinthians 5:21 tells us, "For He made Him who knew no sin to be sin for us, that we might become the righteousness of God in Him." Paul is emphasizing that, everything we do, we should do from the standpoint that we are in right-standing with God. Every time Satan brings accusation, guilt, and condemnation, we have to respond by saying, "There is therefore now no condemnation to those who are in Christ Jesus... for the law of the Spirit of life in Christ Jesus has made me free from the law of sin and death," and I am found in Him "not having a righteousness, which is from the law, but that which is through faith in Christ, the righteousness which is from God by faith" (Romans 8:1; Philippians 3:9).

It is this righteousness that serves as our breastplate. First Thessalonians 5:8 describes it as a breastplate of faith and love. That's true. From man's side, righteousness is by faith. On God's side, righteousness is given to the believer by Jesus' love. One of our family friend and mentor, Pastor Timothy John, says that a person who has the breastplate of righteousness is a person whose past is pardoned and who has peace for the present, plans for the future, and power to progress.

When a person begins to acknowledge what Jesus has done for him on the cross of Calvary and begins to confess it (bringing his spirit, soul, and body in agreement by the words of his mouth), the righteousness of God is put on. It moves from a positional promise to an experiential one fulfilled. It moves from imputed righteousness to imparted righteousness. It moves from something that has been done legally to a place where you are experiencing the power of righteousness working in you, for you, and through you. So go ahead and put on the breastplate of righteousness.

# Chapter 13

# The Shoes of Peace

*"And having shod your feet in preparation to face the enemy with the firm-footed stability, the promptness and the readiness produced by the good news of the Gospel of Peace"* (Ephesians 6:15, AMP).

*"Therefore, having been justified by faith, we have peace with God through our Lord Jesus Christ"* (Romans 5:1).

*"And by Him to reconcile all things to Himself, by Him, whether things on earth or things in heaven, having made peace through the blood of His cross"* (Colossians 1:20).

*"For He Himself is our peace, who has made both one, and has broken down the middle wall of separation, having abolished in His flesh the enmity, that is, the law of commandments contained in ordinances, so as to create in Himself one new man from the two, thus making peace"* (Ephesians 2:14–15).

Imagine yourself standing barefooted in a rocky terrain, like in the Middle East. You could move ever so carefully, but without shoes you would be useless in battle on such terrain. The weight of the other pieces of armor would only make your feet more sensitive if you had no protection. You would be a "push-over" for the enemy, as you would have no agility and would be wincing in pain every time you attempted to move. This is why it is essential to have our "feet shod with the gospel of peace."

The provisions made for the Roman soldier were not boots but sandals. The sandals provided the soldier with a sure grip, to prevent his sliding, slipping, and falling. In those days, a very familiar device used on the battleground was to place certain traps or stakes hiding in the ground. These stakes would be made of shard wood with a narrow point and would stick up slightly above the surface, almost invisible. Many times, the enemy would come on the field, and if individuals didn't have their feet braced, these stakes would go inside their feet, and the feet would become infected. So, the soldier's shoes were very important. We may look at shoes today and err in thinking they are of little importance, or maybe we could look at another piece of armor and underestimate its importance. Please understand every piece of the armor is important.

The Bible connects shoes with peace because shoes represent the way of a person, his lifestyle or manner. Paul is encouraging us by saying God is going to make us stand in peace in the midst of warfare. Furthermore, the Hebrew word for peace is *shalom*. It gives us the idea of completeness, soundness, and security. Its Greek equal is *eirene* which gives us the idea of rest or is the opposite of disturbance. When we stand in peace, then we stand in rest, in completeness, in soundness, and in security. Peace is also the ability to keep silent when abused, criticized, slandered, misjudged, or even angry. We use the expression, "To hold one's peace," which means someone chooses to keep silent.

Whichever way we define it, peace is the material for our shoes. The fallen man in Adam had lost peace with God, but because of Jesus Christ he has peace with God. It is in this peace that the Christian soldier stands shod and ready to face the enemy.

The Scriptures give us three benefits of the peace of God.

- Peace of God brings wholeness—"'Peace I leave with you, My peace I give to you; not as the world gives do I give to you. Let not your heart be troubled, neither let it be afraid'"

(John 14:27). "Now may the God of peace Himself sanctify you completely; and may your whole spirit, soul, and body be preserved blameless at the coming of our Lord Jesus Christ" (1 Thessalonians 5:23). "Now may the Lord of peace Himself give you peace always in every way. The Lord be with you all" (2 Thessalonians 3:16).

- Peace of God rules the heart—"And let the peace of God rule in your hearts, to which also you were called in one body; and be thankful" (Colossians 3:15).
- Peace of God guards the mind—"And the peace of God, which surpasses all understanding, will guard your hearts and minds through Christ Jesus" (Philippians 4:7). "You will keep him in perfect peace, whose mind is stayed on You, because he trusts in You" (Isaiah 26:3

Although we all want the benefits of God's peace, the truth is we face daily the very enemies of Peace. They are:

- **An unrenewed mind.** A mind that is not renewed daily by the Word of God is a disturbed, anxious, doubtful, fearful, and worrisome place. An unrenewed mind is a place where the peace of God is absent.
- **Unforgiveness.** When a person harbors unforgiveness in her life, she cannot experience the peace of God. It affects every part of her life. It affects her prayers, relationships with people, and relationship with God. Jesus told us to forgive others so that we can receive forgiveness from Him (Mark 11:25).
- **Offenses and bitterness.** In Matthew 5:23–25, Jesus told us to be reconciled to our brother before we bring our gifts to God. There seems an urgency in these verses to take care to address offenses and be reconciled. The writer of Hebrews told us to be careful "lest anyone fall short of the grace of God; lest any root of bitterness springing up cause trouble, and by this many become defiled" (Hebrews 12:15). The Apostle Paul said, "'This being so, I myself always strive to have a conscience without offense toward God and men'" (Acts 24:16).

- **Anger.** Paul told us to put anger away. "Let all bitterness, wrath, anger, clamor, and evil speaking be put away from you, with all malice" (Ephesians 4:31). He also told us to put it off as if taking off a garment. "But now you yourselves are to put off all these: anger, wrath, malice, blasphemy, filthy language out of your mouth" (Colossians 3:8).

Now that we understand peace a little more, let's look at the reference to our shoes. When the Apostle Paul uses the shoe analogy, there are three things I think about shoes that speak to me of their significance in warfare:

- Shoes speak of readiness. This means that, when the enemy comes to attack, we should not be caught unaware. When we face surprise attacks, we don't loose our minds or get angry. Since we are deeply rooted in the peace of God, we'll stand in that same peace. Nothing, then, should come as a surprise, thus causing us to respond in a negative manner. We are ready for any news.
- Shoes speak of stability. The peace of God produces stability. It gives us firm-footing. We will not be able to slip or fall when the enemy has hidden agendas.
- Shoes speak of mobility. Nothing is more important in an army than mobility. Paul is saying, "Move forward in the peace of God, in the security, the completeness of God's plan and purpose." When an army is mobile, the enemy always attacks where the army has been and never where it is. Shoes of peace cause us to progress in the plan of God.

# Chapter 14

# The Shield of Faith

*"Above all, taking the shield of faith with which you will be able to quench all the fiery darts of the wicked one"* (Ephesians 6:16).

*"In every battle you will need faith as your shield to stop the fiery arrows aimed at you by Satan"* (Ephesians 6:16, LB).

*"Unbelief puts our circumstance between us and God, but faith puts God between us and our circumstances"* (F.B. Meyer).

Having come to the fourth piece of armor listed, we find that Paul changes the pattern of his language. In talking about the belt of truth, the breastplate of righteousness, and the shoes of peace, he uses the word, "having." Now coming to the shield of faith, the helmet of salvation, and the sword of the Spirit he uses the term, "take." The reason for the change in the language is because the first three portions of the armor are fixed to the body by a special fastening. The belt is fastened as are the breastplate and sandals. These next three pieces of armor are not fixed to the body. They are not attached.

When a soldier is in the barracks or in the camp, the first three pieces of the armor are always on. The second set of the armor only needs to be in hand when marching towards battle. If the soldier is sitting down in the tent, taking a rest, he still has the breastplate on, the belt on, but his sword, helmet, and shield are not needed and, therefore, not in use. When the alarm or trumpet sounds, he quickly takes the helmet, the shield, and the sword and marches to fight. So Paul here says, "Take the shield of faith."

The text begins with the phrase, "Above all." Above all does not mean the most important thing is to take the shield. Paul is saying to take these next pieces, too, or in addition to the other pieces.

Paul relates the shield with faith because a shield covered the whole body. In the similar manner, faith is required for every area of our lives. A Roman soldier was considered a laughingstock if he lost his shield. Either the soldier brought the shield home with him, or he was brought home upon it.

The Scriptures record three different types of shields—namely, a buckler, a door shield, and a tower shield. Let me take them in order here.

A buckler is a round shield strapped to the arm of a soldier. It was very lightweight and mostly used in hand-to-hand combat. Second Samuel 22:31 refers to this type of shield in reference to God: "As for God, His way is perfect; the word of the LORD is proven; He is a shield to all who trust in Him."

A door shield covered the entire body. The soldier could hide entirely behind it. A tower shield was similar to the door shield. But the use of this was different. The soldier used the tower shield by standing shoulder-to-shoulder to build a protective wall against the arrows of the enemy.

So a shield of faith constituted that the entire body be protected by it. In the same manner, faith is to cover our entire body, our entire lives, not just a particular area. On a daily basis, we need to learn to develop faith in every area of our lives. Many have faith for finances but don't have faith for healing of their sick body. I know so many people who, if they have financial trouble, are not worried at all because they have developed faith to believe God's Word and operate the principles of sowing and reaping to see results. But the same people cannot even get a headache healed. Why? Because they have developed faith for finances, but failed to develop faith for healing.

John declared that our faith overcomes the world—"For whatever is born of God overcomes the world. And this is the victory that has overcome the world—our faith" (1 John 5:4). John Paten, a missionary to South Sea Islanders, could find no corresponding island words for believe, trust, or have faith. The natives didn't have one. One day he heard an islander say, "It's so good to rest my whole weight on this chair." This became his word for faith—resting one's whole weight upon it. Faith used in our main text means the ability to apply quickly what the Word of God declares. It means to repel everything the devil does or attempts to do to us. We, then, wholly rest our weight upon God's Word.

Another thing about the shield is it's mobile. You can move it around and guard yourself from any direction the darts or arrows are coming. Paul compares Satan's attacks to fiery darts. We addressed the different darts in a previous chapter. When Satan shoots his darts against our relationships, finances, calling, etc., we need to learn to hold up the shield of faith in that area.

During Paul's days, the arrows were made of either wood or metal. The sharp, pointed arrow was covered with a flammable substance. When the arrows were fired, they would ignite this material so that it would burst into flames, and each arrow would help penetrate the target or any type of shield. So it is with the devil, he constantly fires flammable arrows at us. Isn't it amazing that when we wake up in the morning we find that before we have had time to do any thinking, thoughts come to us, evil thoughts, and perhaps even blasphemous thoughts? These are fiery darts, and this is what Paul is talking about. Hold your shield of faith against those darts and don't only be on the offensive, use God's Word and become defensive in your daily fight.

The Shield is unique in that it is armor used to protect other armor. It keeps the arrows from the helmet and from the head. Don't underestimate the value given to the shield. In old times, the shield was prized by a soldier above all other pieces of armor. As I mentioned earlier, he counted it a great shame to lose his shield—

even a greater shame than losing the battle. Therefore, he would not part with it even when he was under heavy attack but esteemed it an honor to die with his shield in his hand. Mother's would charge their sons who became soldiers to fight for their country by saying, "Either bring your shield home with you or be brought home upon your shield." A mother would rather see her son dead with his shield than alive without it. So esteem your faith highly. Paul in describing the armor doesn't tell us what to do with the belt or the breastplate, but he does tell us what to do with our shields—quench those fiery darts of the enemy.

The 'fiery darts' have 3 common characteristics

### 1. Darts are Swift

Satan needs no more than a blink of a eye and his temptations, evil thoughts, impure attitudes are right there. David looks upon Bathsheba and the devil's arrow is in his heart before he can close his window. The Psalmist compares the darts (God's arrows) to lightning.

Psalm 18:14 "He sent out His arrows and scattered the foe, Lightnings in abundance, and He vanquished them"

### 2. Darts fly secretly with no noise at the wrong time, and out of nowhere.

The Bible says in Psalm that the wicked shoot their arrows in secret. Psalm 64:4 "that they may shoot in secret at the blameless; Suddenly they shoot at him and do not fear." Usually the reason it is secretly is because it came from unexpected people. Satan will use closest to you to pull you down, discourage you, and distract you. He will use your husbands tongue. He will use your children to get you upset. If you don't think so, just think who would have ever suspected that Abraham the great man of faith would be Satan's instrument to betray his wife into the hands of sin? The devil is so deceptive and secretive that he makes a BOW that looks like God's BOW to shoot his arrows and the believer thinks it is God who is chastening him. Job cried out because of the 'arrows of the Almighty' and their 'poison' (Job 6:4) but all the time Satan was practicing his wickedness upon him.

3. Darts wound, but lead to death

Many darts or arrows that were fired were not only prepared with flammable material to produce fire and explode, but it was covered with poison like chemical. The reason for this was when an enemy was shot, many times the person would just pull out the arrow and continue. There was not much harm because of distance or speed. But when this poison is gone in the body, it will slowly kill. It's the same way with the darts of the devil. The devil will send temptations and deception to kill us slowly. Satan makes you think, "Look I only have impure thoughts, after all we are humans, nothing happened, so it's ok to have these kinds of thoughts off and on" We begin to think like that, and after doing it over and over, we can't control and renew our minds according to the Word of God. We are constantly in confusion, distractions, and frustration. The Darts kill softly and secretly. Therefore raise your SHIELD of FAITH and stand victorious.

The Book of Psalms gives us great descriptions about shields. Let's look at these verses as they provide insight about the shield we wield.

- The shield is a gift—"You have also given me the shield of Your salvation; Your right hand has held me up, Your gentleness has made me great" (Psalm 18:35).
- It is a tested shield—"The LORD is my strength and my shield; my heart trusted in Him, and I am helped; therefore my heart greatly rejoices, and with my song I will praise Him" (Psalm 28:7).
- It is an anointed shield—"O God, behold our shield, and look upon the face of Your anointed" (Psalm 84:9).
- It is a surrounding shield—"For You, O LORD, will bless the righteous; with favor You will surround him as with a shield" (Psalm 5:12).
- It is a personal shield—"But You, O LORD, are a shield for me, my glory and the One who lifts up my head" (Psalm 3:3).
- His truth is the power of the shield—"He shall cover you with His feathers, and under His wings you shall take refuge; His truth shall be your shield and buckler" (Psalm 91:4).

- It is a victorious shield—"Do not slay them, lest my people forget; scatter them by Your power, and bring them down, O LORD our shield" (Psalm 59:11).

# Chapter 15

# The Helmet of Salvation

*"And take the helmet of salvation..."* (Ephesians 6:17).

We now come to the fifth piece of armor—the helmet. In the natural, the helmet protects the head. In the spirit, the helmet protects the soul, for in Scripture the word, "mind," is used instead of soul. For centuries, there has been a battle over who will control the thought processes of man's mind. Please understand that every part of the soldier needs to be protected. There is not one part more important than the other. Please note that no one piece of the armour is more important than the other. All the pieces are of vital importance. The enemy is constantly seeking whom he may devour. If we leave any areas open, he will use the opportunity.

Let's look at this word, "soul," as the object of the helmet's protection. Soul addresses the whole person. For example, Jesus said in Mark 8:36, "'For what will it profit a man if he gains the whole world, and loses his own soul?'" Here Jesus is referring to a person's soul, a person's whole self. Our souls are comprised of our whole selves—our minds, our intellects, our very beings. The Apostle John wrote, "Beloved, I pray that you may prosper in all things and be in health, just as your soul prospers" (3 John 1:2).

It's the helmet of salvation, then, that protects the soul or the mind. Now when we study the Scripture, we find the soul is made up of the following five things:

- Will
- Intellect
- Emotions
- Imaginations
- Memory

So the helmet protects the will, the intellect, the emotions, the imaginations, and the memory. For the purpose of our discussion here, I will use 'soul' any time I am referring to these five areas.

## The Will

The human will is sovereign. God will not violate it. We cannot make wrong decisions and then blame God. It doesn't matter whether you are born again or not; the human will has the final say in any decision it makes. If you are born again, you have the joy of merging the human will with the will of God. The greatest experience you will have is when your will is linked with the will of God your Father. In this, no enemy can stand against you; no attack can overcome you; no disease can destroy you.

Each area of the soul works together. How does it do this? Just imagine you are on diet to lose some weight, you're at a friend's house, and you've finished eating. It is time for the dessert, and you know you should not have any sweets at all when suddenly they bring out the New York Style Cheesecake with strawberry topping. Oh, no! It's the end of the diet for you! Suddenly your IMAGINATION gives you the image of the cake with fresh strawberries and whipped cream. Next, your MEMORY kicks in and says, "I had this before at the office party last month; remember how rich it was?" Then, the EMOTIONS come into play, "You know how you enjoyed it. You just loved every bite." The INTELLECT in conjunction with the emotions sends signals all over your body. The eyes focus on the cake, the mouth begins to water, the stomach is making room, and then the WILL steps in and says, "No! You're on a diet!" That ends everything right there! While all the other areas of the soul rebel, the will makes everybody line up or the will can cave in.

Joseph is a great example of somebody whose will was made strong by God's Word and Spirit. While Joseph was in the palace,

Joseph's master's wife continually tempted him to fall into sin with her. Many people get the picture that it happened only in one day. But Genesis 39:10 says, "So it was, as she spoke to Joseph day by day, that he did not heed her, to lie with her or to be with her." See the phrase "day by day." This wasn't just a one-day event. How like the enemy who continually pounds on our wills to submit to him. We need to consistently receive strength from God's Word and the Holy Spirit and stand against the schemes of the devil. Joseph fused his will to the will of God. Your will needs to be disciplined and trained by the Word of God.

## The Intellect

The fastest, the most efficient, and the most productive computer in the world is the human brain. No scientist or medical doctor is able to explain how a small mass of tissue can retain and understand knowledge. The intellect is the place where knowledge is stored, and it is what controls the signals sent to the body. Isaiah 1:18 addresses the intellect when it says, "'Come now, and let us reason together,' says the LORD, 'Though your sins are like scarlet, they shall be as white as snow; though they are red like crimson, they shall be as wool.'"

## Emotions

Emotions are built into every person by God. It is not wrong for you to have emotions. It is wrong for emotions to have you. Many times our emotions are not disciplined and controlled by the Word of God. Emotions add color to our lives. Our lives are not to be led by our emotions, however. We are to be led by the Spirit of God. Some people use their emotions to control and manipulate others. In renewing our minds or souls, we need to constantly renew our emotions, submitting them to the pattern of God's Word. Emotions can either destroy our destinies or simply add color to them. Use the Word of God to direct them towards the abundant life promised in Jesus Christ.

## Imaginations

Someone once said, the greatest nation in the world, is IMAGI-NATION. Our imagination has the creative ability to do anything for God. Imagination is vision, pictures, dreams, and reality that need to be controlled by the Word of God. The enemy corrupts the soul of a person through negative imaginations or images. Imaginations direct our emotions. It is important that we allow the word of God to produce Godly images or imaginations.

## Memory

One of the most important function of the soul is its memory. The memory serves as our point of reference for every thought we have. For many, the hardest area to deal with in their souls is their memory. We are tempted to remember those things we should have forgiven and forgotten. We are aided as we remember God's truth and His manifold blessing in our lives. God is a God who fills the memory with His acts.

Now that we see these five aspects of the soul, why does Paul connect the helmet with salvation? Because the helmet protects the head—the place of leadership—which is the soul. But what is the connection with salvation? In order to rightly answer this question, we must address three aspects of salvation.

The Greek word for salvation is *soteria*, which means deliverance, to be made whole, etc. Paul in 2 Corinthians 1:10 makes this statement regarding salvation, "who delivered us from so great a death, and does deliver us; in whom we trust that He will still deliver us."

Here we have the three tenses of salvation or deliverance: past, present, and future. I believe these three tenses apply to the three parts of man—namely, his spirit, soul, and body. Below is an illustration for understanding.

- Spirit    "Hath delivered us"    Past    Justification
- Soul    "Doth Deliver"    Present    Sanctification
- Body    "Will deliver us"    Future    Glorification

So here we realize that when a person accepts Jesus as her Lord and Savior, being born again, then that person's spirit is saved. Her soul and body are not saved, however. That person on a daily basis needs to renew her mind according to the Word of God so that her soul gets saved—delivered—and makes it's way to wholeness. Then in the future, her body which is corruptible will also get saved by its putting on the incorruptible body in heaven.

The helmet of salvation, then, covers our souls. We need to keep our helmets on and renew our minds so as to be transformed into men and women fit for battle. When a soul is renewed daily by the Word of God, the thoughts come in line with His Word. This results in the following:

- Thoughts → Words → Actions → Habits → Lifestyle

If our thoughts are Godly, then our words will be Godly, our actions will be Godly, our habits will be Godly, and our lifestyles will be Godly. If the thoughts are infiltrated by Satan, then the infiltration will be processed all the way through, too. So put on the helmet of salvation and protect your head and so save your soul.

# Chapter 16

# The Sword of the Spirit

*"And take...the sword of the Spirit, which is the word of God"* (Ephesians 6:17).

*"To the Christian armed for defense in battle, the apostle recommends only one weapon of attack; but it is enough, the sword of the Spirit, which is the word of God. It subdues and mortifies evil desires and blasphemous thoughts as they rise within; and answers unbelief and error as they assault from without. A single text, well understood, and rightly applied, at once destroys a temptation or an objection, and subdues the most formidable adversary"* (Matthew Henry).

The sword of the Spirit is the excellent use of the word of God. Peter told us, "For this reason I will not be negligent to remind you always of these things, though you know and are established in the *present truth*" (2 Peter 1:12, emphasis added). The sword of the Spirit is what Jesus used against Satan in the times of His fasting and prayer. Since we have dealt with the sword of the Spirit in the section on the belt of truth, we will look at some things that make the sword dull and how we can sharpen it.

The way to sharpen the sword is to tune our ears to hear what the Holy Spirit is saying. We can read and know God's *Logos* (the living, written Word of God) but never listen or hear what God is actually saying. We can know the Word yet miss the message! Scriptures tell us so many times to take heed to how we hear and to what we hear. Proverbs 28:9, for example, says, "One who turns away his ear from hearing the law, even his prayer is an abomination." And Amos, for just an additional example, says, "'Behold, the days are coming,' says the Lord GOD, that I will send a famine on the land, not a famine of bread, nor a thirst for water, but of hearing the words of the LORD'" (8:11).

Our ability to wield the sword of the Spirit lies in our ability to hear the Word of the Lord, and our ability to hear the Word of the Lord depends on the condition of our ears. The Bible addresses different ear conditions.

## Itching Ears

II Timothy 4:3 *"For the time will come when they will not endure sound doctrine, but according to their own desires, because they have itching ears, they will heap up for themselves teachers"*

What are itching ears? Itching ears speak of people who want to hear things that will satisfy their own personal drives and lusts. They have ideas and then they go to preachers, prophets, and God's Word to validate those things instead of letting God's Word direct them. Many preachers also begin to preach only what sells, only what the crowd likes to hear. They don't want to endure sound doctrine as 2 Timothy 4:3 says—"For the time will come when they will not endure sound doctrine, but according to their own desires, because they have itching ears, they will heap up for themselves teachers." Such individuals may say we need to change with the times. I agree we need to change with the times, but we always have to remember we can keep changing methods but never God's Word. We have to hear what the Spirit is saying to us even if it doesn't fit into the mainstream of what others are saying.

## Uncircumcised Ears

Jeremiah 4 addresses the men of Judah and Jerusalem as their hearts had become cluttered with the things of the world. "Break up your fallow ground, and do not sow among thorns. Circumcise yourselves to the Lord, and take away the foreskins of your hearts, you men of Judah and inhabitants of Jerusalem, lest My fury come forth like fire, and burn so that no one can quench it, because of the evil of your doings'" (4:3–). They wanted to walk on both sides of the fence. There was no total commitment. There was compromise in their lives. Compromise dulls the sword more than anything. We clean the heart, we heal the ears, and in turn hear what the Spirit is saying.

## Stubborn Ears

Stubborn ears are products of rebellion and self-centeredness. People with stubborn ears have not learned to submit to Christ and to one another in the Body of Christ. They live for themselves. The Word of the Lord came to the prophet Zechariah concerning a people who had refused to hear the Word of the Lord. They "'shrugged their shoulders, and stopped their ears so that they could not hear. Yes, they made their hearts like flint, refusing to hear the law and the words which the LORD of hosts had sent by His Spirit through the former prophets. Thus great wrath came from the LORD of hosts'" (7:11–12).

## Dull Ears

Continual disobedience to what God is saying will create a distance between you and Him. In fact, it will cause your ears to become dull and your sword to become dull. As Hebrews 5:11 says, "Of whom we have much to say, and hard to explain, since you have become dull of hearing."

## Forgetful Ears

James 1:22 warns people to not only be hearers of the Word but to be doers. Verses 23–25 continue the thought, "For if anyone is a hearer of the word and not a doer, he is like a man observing his natural face in a mirror; for he observes himself, goes away, and immediately forgets what kind of man he was. But he who looks into the perfect law of liberty and continues in it, and is not a forgetful hearer but a doer of the work, this one will be blessed in what he does."

This speaks about people who have no priority in life. They hear what God is saying to them and they know it's the truth, but do not use their time to apply the changes in their lives that the Word requires. They don't have the discipline to bring His priorities into their lives. They have heard the truth, but now have forgotten it because there is no value for it.

## Faithless Ears

Hebrews 4:2 reads, "For indeed the gospel was preached to us as well as to them; but the word which they heard did not profit them, not being mixed with faith in those who heard it." This speaks of people who do not have faith to mix with what they are hearing. Their ears, indeed, are faithless as is their hearing.

In the above 6 references, we have discussed things that will cause your sword to be dull, once taken care of it will heal your ears and sharpen your sword.

# Chapter 17

# Put the Armor on with Prayer

*"Praying always with all prayer and supplication in the Spirit, being watchful to this end with all perseverance and supplication for all the saints"* (Ephesians 6:18).

*"Pray at all time—on every occasion, in every season—in the Spirit, with all (manner of) prayer and entreaty. To that end keep alert and watch with strong purpose and perseverance, interceding in behalf of all the saints (God's consecrated people)"* (Ephesians 6:18, AMP).

*"Much prayer, much revival, little prayer, little revival"* (Jonathan Edwards).

*"There has never been a spiritual awakening in any country or locally that did not begin in united prayer"* (A.T. Pierson).

A soldier on his knees in prayer is the most powerful stance he can take. Prayer is not a add-on to the armor, rather it is woven in and through the armor. Some have taken this verse to mean that Paul is still dealing with the whole armor of God and that he is saying the next piece is prayer. I disagree. Some have even suggested that praying with all prayer and supplication in the Spirit means that you use the sword of the Spirit by praying in the Spirit. This I believe to be inaccurate. I believe Paul is saying to put on the whole armor of God, and before putting on the armor pray; while putting on the armor, pray; and after you have it on, pray. There are some old hymns which paint an exact picture of this verse.

> Put on the Gospel armor,
> Each Piece put on with prayer.
>
> To keep your armor bright
> Attend with constant care;
> Still walking in your Captain's sight,
> And watching unto prayer.

The Bible outlines many different types of prayer. Remember one of the things that the Apostle Paul emphasized is that the prayer be with supplication and in the Spirit. Supplication simply means an ongoing request for a given matter to be settled in God's will. We understand in the Spirit simply means in partnership with the Holy Spirit. So as we move on, remember that we are to continually pray in partnership with the Holy Spirit till the matter which lines up with God's will is settled.

The Bible outlines many types of prayer, too. We shall not study all the avenues of prayer, but just one or two types which will help us in spiritual warfare. For more study, I have written about prayer in my first book, *Believer's Mandate—Foundation for Abundant Life*. For our present discussion, however, let's look back at Paul's exhortation to pray with ALL prayers. The Bible mentions different types of prayers. Here are those I believe are relevant to our spiritual warfare.

## Prayer of Binding and Loosing

Jesus said, "'Verily I say unto you, whatsoever ye shall bind on earth shall be bound in heaven: and whatsoever ye shall loose on earth shall be loosed in heaven'" (Matthew 18:18). Binding means to restrict, to limit, to tie up, to hinder, to prevent, to restrain, to stop action, or to entangle.

The Scriptures commands us to bind:
- Satan;
- Demons or evil spirits;
- Principalities and evil powers;
- Actions and attitudes of People;
- Sickness and disease;
- Assignments of Satan towards people's lives through witch-craft, etc.; and
- Works of the flesh.

Loosing is the opposite of binding. It means to untie, to release, to allow, to cancel, to forgive, to set free, to permit, to liberate. So when we put the definition in the verse we can say that the purpose is to restrict (restrain, limit, tie, hinder, prevent, stop, entangle) on earth those things that are restricted in heaven, and to release (untie, forgive, cancel, allow, set free, permit, liberate) on earth those things that are released in heaven. We have been authorized to bind what God binds and loose what Satan binds or to loose what God looses and bind what Satan looses.

The Scriptures command us to loose:
- People who have been bound with sickness;
- People who have been bound with disease (fear, sin, etc.);
- People who have been bound with evil habits (lust, greed, etc.);
- People who have been bound with controlling powers in relationships; and
- People who have been bound by curses.

## Prayer of Agreement

Jesus said verse 19 of Matthew 18, "'Again I say to you that if two of you agree on earth concerning anything that they ask, it will be done for them by My Father in heaven.'" We call this the prayer of agreement. So, when a husband and wife, when a family, when two or more believers pray together in agreement, Jesus promised what they prayed for would be done!

## Prayer of Commitment and Consecration

In Hebrews 10:7, the writer says that when Jesus came into the world He said, "'Behold, I have come—in the volume of the book it is written of Me—to do Your will, O God.'" I believe this is the prayer that Jesus prayed daily. We should pray such prayers of commitment and consecration. We need to daily consecrate ourselves to our Master.

## Prayer of Faith

Jesus told us in Mark 11:22 to have faith in God. We know from Hebrews that we cannot please God unless we have faith. But back in Mark 11, Jesus said, "'For assuredly, I say to you, whoever says to this mountain, "Be removed and be cast into the sea," and does not doubt in his heart, but believes that those things he says will be done, he will have whatever he says. Therefore I say to you, whatever things you ask when you pray, believe that you receive them, and you will have them'" (23–24). When we pray, we are to pray in faith believing that we'll receive, and we will receive it.

## Prayer of Thanksgiving

Paul encourages Timothy that a thanksgiving prayer be made on behalf of people—"Therefore I exhort first of all that supplications, prayers, intercessions, and giving of thanks be made for all men" (1 Timothy 2:1). We are also told in Ephesians 5:20 always to give thanks to God for all things, and we are told in 1 Thessalonians 5:18 to give thanks in everything—that's for everything and in everything! Many times God tells us to thank Him in faith for the answer. Thanksgiving has great promise.

## Prayer of Intercession or Intercessory Prayer

Intercession is simply praying on behalf of another. It can mean to come in between. In between simply means that you are standing in between the person, place, region, or country and God. You are praying for God's will to be settled in the person, region, church, country, etc. Looking back at 1 Timothy 2:1, we are told to intercede for all men.

148

Jesus is our Chief Intercessor in that "He always lives to make intercession" for us (Hebrews 7:25). He lived a sinless life on our behalf. He died on the cross on our behalf. On the cross, Jesus didn't win the victory for Himself, for He was already victorious. He won the victory for us.

We shall discuss in fuller detail the prayer of intercession or intercessory prayer later on.

## Praying in the Holy Spirit or Tongues

Paul exhorted the Corinthian believers to pray with the spirit and with understanding (1 Corinthians 14:13). This type of prayer with the spirit is praying in the Holy Spirit or praying in tongues. Earlier in that same chapter, Paul said, "For he who speaks in a tongue does not speak to men but to God, for no one understands him; however, in the spirit he speaks mysteries" (2). You see, he was saying that speaking in tongues is a way to pray, a way to talk to God. For more study, I have written about praying in the Holy Spirit in my first book, *Believer's Mandate — Foundation for Abundant Life*.

# PART IV

# Satan's Weapons

# Chapter 18

# The Weapon of Temptation

*"Let no one say when he is tempted, 'I am tempted by God'; for God cannot be tempted by evil, nor does He Himself tempt anyone"* (James 1:13).

E very soldier must understand the nature of his enemy. He must be prepared to know his enemy's disguises and recognize his camouflage. Enemy spies many times disguise their faces to hide their identity. We should not be surprised to learn, therefore, that Satan disguises himself as an angel of light and his followers pretend to be servants of righteousness (2 Corinthians 11:14–15). So it's important to know and study our opponent. If we are in war, then we should learn something about this enemy, his weapons, his tactics, his strategies.

In every place today, satanic activity has increased. First Timothy 4:1–3 warns us that in the last days people would depart from the faith and give heed to seducing spirits and to doctrines of the devils. Studying the Scriptures, we find seven main weapons Satan uses in his attack against believers. Of course there are many weapons the enemy uses, but we will focus on these primary ones. They are temptation, accusation, deception, mixture, affliction, intimidation, and rebellion. In this chapter, we are focusing on Satan's weapon of temptation

# Temptation

To tempt someone is to entice or allure them. Temptation, then, is something enticing or alluring. Biblical examples of temptation are found in Matthew 4:1, Mark 1:13, 1 Corinthians 7:5, John 14:30, and 1 John 5:18.

Temptation is quite easy to understand because everybody faces it. Whether you are a child, a teenager, young adult, and a married person, you will face temptation at some point. There is a story told about a little boy in a grocery store that I think illustrates the nature of temptation. The boy was standing near an open box of peanut butter cookies. "Now then, young man," said the grocer as he approached the boy, "What are you up to?"

"Nothing," replied the boy. "Nothing."

"Well it looks to me like you were trying to take a cookie."

"You're wrong, mister, I'm trying *not* to!"

Well, my friend, that's temptation! We understand temptation leads to trouble. Such was the plight of a man I read about in *Reader's Digest*. This man said he was shopping in the mall with his wife when a shapely young woman in a short, form-fitting dress walked by. He said as she walked by his eyes followed her. Without looking up from the item she was examining, his wife asked, "Was it worth the trouble that you are now in?"

We face temptation consistently in life. But it's wonderful to be reminded of Hebrews 4:15, which says, "For we do not have a High Priest who cannot sympathize with our weaknesses, but was in all points tempted as we are, yet without sin." You see, Jesus was tempted in all points, but still His life was without sin. Facing temptation is not sin, but agreeing and giving into that temptation will of course lead to sin. There are two significant times when Satan tempted Jesus—once while in the wilderness and the other at the time of His passion. Yet Jesus did not succumb to Satan's weapon.

Any discussion of temptation must address that the Bible always differentiates between tests and temptation. Many versions of the Bible use these words to mean the same thing, but that is not correct. God tests believers. Testing is there to build perseverance and character; it's used by the Lord to prove His servants. God doesn't test us to find out how we will respond in a situation because He already knows how we will respond. The testing is for us—so that we'll know how we respond.

You see, testing is a mirror that shows us our character, ability, strength, etc. James 1:13 reads, "Let no one say when he is tempted, 'I am tempted by God'; for God cannot be tempted by evil, nor does He Himself tempt anyone." Satan tempts; God tests. Temptation is a road leading to death. Remember there is no temptation that you cannot overcome. When you are walking with God, God is controlling everything in your life. Now if you are already living in disobedience to God, Satan will take you deeper in bondage through temptation. But be encouraged by 1 Corinthians 10:13 — "No temptation has overtaken you except such as is common to man; but God is faithful, who will not allow you to be tempted beyond what you are able, but with the temptation will also make the way of escape, that you may be able to bear it." That's a promise to stand upon when confronted with temptation.

But here are some things we must remember about Satan and how he uses his weapon of temptation.

## Satan's Timing

Satan chooses when to tempt the believer. Ecclesiastes 3:1 helps us understand that "to everything there is a time and a season." Please understand that Satan is always ready to tempt you and to bring you into the bondage of sin so as to destroy you. When we study the Scriptures, we find many times he'll use temptation as a device to bring you down. Let's look at some of these times so we can be alert and ready for his attack.

Satan tempts us in times of isolation. David was at the rooftop of his palace. He should have been with his army. Joseph went to Potiphar's house to do business when no one else was there (except, of course, Potiphar's wife) he was faced with temptation. Jesus was alone in the wilderness, without the crowds or His disciples.

Satan tempts us in times of fruitfulness. Joseph was progressing in his life and obedience to God. He was receiving favor from Potiphar at the time of Satan's temptation, but he overcame.

Satan tempts us after a great victory. Look at the children of Israel after the destruction of Jericho. They were promised a mighty victory, which they received. However, they were told not to take any plunder, but Satan tempted Achan, and he coveted and took the spoil.

## Satan's Chosen Vessels

Often, Satan chooses people to succumb to temptation. Proverbs 1:10 tells us, "My son, if sinners entice you, do not consent." For Job his own wife said to him, "'Curse God and die.'" For Joseph it was Potiphar's wife. Please understand this wasn't just about sleeping one night with her. Joseph could have used this opportunity to move up closer to Pharaoh, but this was Satan's plan not God's.

## Temptation's Choice

You have a choice! That's right! Temptation offers you a choice, and you do not have to choose to yield yourself to it. James tells us, "Blessed is the man who endures temptation" (1:12). If Christ was tempted and He was found without sin, then we can follow His example and not fall into temptation. We must:

- Remember temptation is a choice that exposes our hearts— "Every man is tempted when he is drawn away of his own lust, and enticed" (James 1:14).
- Understand Satan never tempts us to do what we cannot do; he always tempts us to do things we are capable of doing. Jesus could have turned the stones into bread after the time of His fasting.
- I heard one preacher say, "I believe after the resurrection when the disciples were on the beach and had nothing to eat and Jesus showed up and ask have ye nothing to eat. I believe, he took some stones and turned it into bread. Jesus did this to tell Satan I can do it when I want to, not when you (Satan) want it done".
- Realize God has wisdom in handling your temptation— "The Lord knows how to deliver the godly out of temptations" (2 Peter 2:9).
- Realize Christ prays for us to overcome temptation—"He is also able to save to the uttermost those who come to God

through Him, since He always lives to make intercession for them" (Hebrews 7:25).

- Pray for ourselves as Jesus taught His disciples—"'And do not lead us into temptation, but deliver us from the evil one'" (Matthew 6:13).

# Chapter 19

# The Weapon of Accusation

*"Then I heard a loud voice saying in heaven, 'Now salvation, and strength, and the kingdom of our God, and the power of His Christ have come, for the accuser of our brethren, who accused them before our God day and night, has been cast down"* (Revelation 12:10).

*"Then he showed me Joshua the high priest standing before the Angel of the LORD, and Satan standing at his right hand to oppose him. And the LORD said to Satan, 'The LORD rebuke you, Satan! The LORD who has chosen Jerusalem rebuke you! Is this not a brand plucked from the fire?' Now Joshua was clothed with filthy garments, and was standing before the Angel"* (Zechariah 3:1–3).

Every person is very familiar with accusation. Each one of us, at some point in our lives, has been accused of something. It may have been something we were guilty of, or we may have been falsely accused. Such accusation may have been used against us by Satan, the accuser of the brethren. His weapon of accusation is wielded by him and, sometimes, by people he's influencing.

## Accusations from the Devil

In Job 1, we find Satan appeared before God. After God asked Satan if he had considered Job, Satan responded by accusing the man to God, "God, the only reason Job worships You is because You bless him. If You took away Your blessing, Job would curse You." His tactic is the same today. He will accuse us by saying such things as, "You don't read the Bible enough," "You don't pray enough," or some other incriminating statement. We need to remember two things: (1) Jesus is our high priest and our defense attorney. He is standing on our behalf before the Father, defending us. (2) The blood of Jesus Christ continually cleanses us from all the filth of the world. No matter how hard Satan tries to accuse us, the verdict is the same. Father God, justly looking at the evidence presented before Him (His blood and righteousness), pronounces us not guilty, blameless, and above reproach.

## Accusations from People

Facing accusation from people means that someone is pointing out our faults and mistakes for the purpose of hurting us. Proverbs 30:10 says, "Do not malign a servant to his master, lest he curse you, and you be found guilty." God's Word says, "Do not be an accuser." But isn't there a time when we need to point out people's sin? For example, if someone in the leadership of the church is teaching false doctrine, shouldn't you come and tell the pastor? If a member of the church has a problem with anger or gossiping, shouldn't you come and point out this destructive behavior? Maybe. But please consider your action very carefully. Let me give you two reasons why.

Turn with me to 2 Timothy 3:3. Here Paul is a listing of various sins, and in that list is the word "slander." Slander means false accusation. What interests me is that this word in Greek is *diabolos*. This of course in many languages means the devil. To falsely accuse is the most Satan-like thing that we can do. Do you remember Satan in the Garden of Eden? What did he do? He falsely accused God. He tempted Eve by saying that God was really trying to hold something good back from her. So, we must be careful not to bring an accusation against anyone, and we should never bring a false accusation against someone.

Here are a few things to remember when you've been falsely accused by people.

- When you are falsely accused, get several people who are mature and well-trusted. Ask them to weigh the validity of the accusation in the presence of your accusers. Moses wrote, "'Then both men in the controversy shall stand before the LORD, before the priests and the judges who serve in those days. And the judges shall make careful inquiry, and indeed, if the witness is a false witness, who has testified falsely against his brother, then you shall do to him as he thought to have done to his brother; so you shall put away the evil from among you'" (Deuteronomy 19:17–20).

- If need be, bring the accusations to the attention of spiritual leaders. John writes, "Therefore, if I come, I will call to mind his deeds which he does, prating against us with malicious words. And not content with that, he himself does not receive the brethren, and forbids those who wish to, putting them out of the church" (3 John 1:10).

- Ask the Lord to intercede and fight your battles for you. David wrote, "Do not keep silent, O God of my praise! For the mouth of the wicked and the mouth of the deceitful have opened against me; they have spoken against me with a lying tongue. They have also surrounded me with words of hatred, and fought against me without a cause. In return for my love they are my accusers, but I give myself to prayer" (Psalm 109:1–4).

- Remember that returning evil for evil is a trap of the devil. Peter wrote, "Therefore, laying aside all malice, all deceit, hypocrisy, envy, and all evil speaking" (1 Peter 2:1). God has a way of working everything together for the greater good. Ask the Lord to give you a special measure of grace, patience, and confidence that He will right any wrongs that are done to you. His justice is perfect although not hasty.

- Instead of fearing people, choose to fear the Lord and hate evil. Peter wrote to a persecuted church fellowship, "Who, when He was reviled, did not revile in return; when He suffered, He did not threaten, but committed Himself to

Him who judges righteously" (1 Peter 2:23). Although Jesus asserted His rights before His accusers, He resisted the temptation to take vengeance into His own hands. Jesus knew the Lord's mighty power, truth, and wisdom would bring vindication. Jesus bore the cross of shame for the sake of those He loved; we are to follow in His footprints.

- Never accuse anyone on secondhand information
- Never accuse anyone out of anger.
- Remember it is much easier to be critical than to be correct.

So take the harder road and be correct and in line with God's Word. C.S. Lewis once said, "The safest road to hell is the gradual one—the gentle slope, soft underfoot, without sudden turnings, without milestones, without signposts."

# Chapter 20

# The Weapon of Deception

*"But I fear, lest somehow, as the serpent deceived Eve by his craftiness, so your minds may be corrupted from the simplicity that is in Christ"* (2 Corinthians 11:3).

*"So the great dragon was cast out, that serpent of old, called the Devil and Satan, who deceives the whole world; he was cast to the earth, and his angels were cast out with him"* (Revelation 12:9).

Satan is a master deceiver. Deception is one of his strongest weapons. Religions are birthed out of deception. Marriages are broken because of deception. Churches are divided by deception. To deceive carries the idea of being led astray. Every sin is the fruit of a deception.

- I won't get caught. No one will know about this or see me do it.
- This will gratify me. (Temporary gratification is not worth the pain!)
- This will make me happy.
- This will make me rich.
- I can be my own boss.
- I don't have to obey.

Remember the anointing and the Word of God work together to dissolve deception. The Bible warns us this will happen to us if we remain ignorant of the Word of God and fail to put God's protective firewall in service.

Listen to Paul's words in 1 Timothy 4:1: "Now the Spirit expressly says that in latter times some shall depart from the faith, giving heed to deceiving spirits and doctrines of demons." Like viruses on today's Internet, Satan's chief strategy is to plant the counterfeit wherever Christ plants the truth. He wants to mix the tares with the wheat. Therefore, it is important you are able to detect the counterfeit and separate the teachings of Christ from the false teachings of the world. This is, in a sense, your access control policy between you and the network system of the world today. Here are three things that will help in your fight against deception.

## The Anointing of God

First John 2:20 tells us, "But you have an anointing from the Holy One, and you know all things." The anointing of God abides in you, and the Holy Spirit is the one who teaches you the truth. He serves as your gatekeeper and should be your guide into all truth Christ reveals to your heart. Jesus made this clear in John. 14:17 when He said, "'the Spirit of truth, whom the world cannot receive, because it neither sees Him nor knows Him; but you know Him, for He dwells with you and will be in you."

The "anointing" John describes is especially designed to meet the problem of uncertainty in the face of the many deceitful and deceptive concepts that are in the world around you and infiltrating the Church today. Let's look at something else John said, "But the anointing which you have received from Him abides in you, and you do not need for anyone to teach you; but as the same anointing teaches you concerning all things, and is true and is not a lie, and just as it has taught you, you will abide in Him" (1 John 2:27).

How do you know what is the truth? How do you know which interpretation is right about a passage in the Word? The Apostle John says that you have an anointing, abiding in you for that very purpose. It is a spiritual hearing and seeing; it enlightens, strengthens, and opens your ears and eyes of understanding. The Spirit of God wants to guide you into all truth and raise your antenna when it recognizes error if you will tune in and activate His firewall. This anointing of God contains "no lie" because "the Spirit is truth" (1 John 5:6). "Now He who establishes us with you in Christ and has anointed us is God, who also has sealed us and given us the Spirit in our hearts as a guarantee" (2 Corinthians 1:21–22).

# The Teaching Anointing

The Spirit is the Teacher God has given us. Jesus said in John 14:26, "'But the Helper, the Holy Spirit, whom the Father will send in My name, He will teach you all things, and bring to your remembrance all that I said to you.'" Listen again to verse 27 of 1 John 2: "But the anointing which you have received from Him abides in you, and you do not need for anyone to teach you; but as the same anointing teaches you concerning all things, and is true and is not a lie, and just as it has taught you, you will abide in Him."

At first glance, this passage of Scripture seems to contradict other passages in the Bible. You know there are teachers, provided by the Holy Spirit. There is also a gift of teaching. How then could John say, "You have no need for anyone to teach you"? The explanation lies in the level at which this kind of teaching takes place. You know that in literature it is common to use the eye and the ear as metaphors for an inner comprehension of the mind. There are actually three levels of seeing and hearing possible to a human being. First, the eyes and the ears are physical organs designed to see and to hear. Now as physical organs they sometimes malfunction, and you have to provide help for them, such as glasses or contact lenses for the eyes or hearing aids for the ears. But the soul has organs of sight and of hearing, as well.

When we say, "I see," for example, we mean we intellectually understand something or grasp it. We can even say we heard something, meaning we are heeding what was said. Thus, you have heard with the mind and the emotions, the soul. When your firewall against deception is activated, you may sense something is wrong about a thing you hear. You don't know quite what it is, but you know it is there, and you say, "This doesn't sound right to me." You do not mean that there is something wrong with the decibels reaching your ears; you mean there is something wrong with the logic of what you've heard.

There are eyes and ears of the spirit by which you may gain certain flashes of insight and thus come to a fuller understanding of a truth in relationship to other truth. You see the whole thing clearly without the necessity of reasoning it all out. These are the eyes and ears of your spirit. You may have been instructed before you were anointed, but now there is nothing in comparison to the way the anointing teaches you. Job 36:22 puts it this way, "'Who teaches like Him?'" You see an example of this type of teaching in Matthew 13 where our Lord began to give the parables of the kingdom. In verse 13, He said, "'Therefore I speak to them in parables, because seeing they do not see, and hearing they do not hear, nor do they understand.'" Do you see the three levels there? Seeing (with their physical eyes), they did not see (with their mental eyes), and hearing (with their physical ears), they did not hear (with their mental ears), nor did they understand (i.e., it does not reach the level of the spirit where they grasp the full meaning of the truth in relationship to themselves and the world around them).

In Matthew 13:16 Jesus said to His disciples, "'But blessed are your eyes for they see, and your ears for they hear.'" But He does not go on to say, "Blessed are you, for you understand." No, they did not understand. They did not grasp yet the whole of what He said to them. They had not yet received the Holy Spirit, and they did not understand His full meaning although they knew intellectually what He was talking about. Listen to what Paul prayed in his great letter to the church at Ephesus: "[I] do not cease to give thanks for you, making mention of you in my prayers: that the God of our Lord Jesus Christ, the Father of glory, may give to you the spirit of wisdom and revelation in the knowledge of Him, the eyes of your understanding being enlightened; that you may know what is the hope of His calling" (1:16–18). The operation of the Holy Spirit is required to understand, to grasp, the immensity of these tremendous things, to be thrilled and gripped with the excitement of what God has set before you. This then is why you do not have any need of human teachers.

At this level, only God can bring such revelation. Only the Spirit of God can touch the human spirit and give insight to it. That is why at this level no human being can help you, although the Holy Spirit will often base His teaching upon the Word, which the human teacher brings. There is a clear example of this in Matthew 16 when our Lord asked his disciples, "Who do men say that the Son of man is?" They named various ones, and then He said, "But who do you say that I am?" Simon Peter replied, "You are the Christ, the Son of the living God." Now Peter had been observing the Lord, but he was puzzled by Him, as all these disciples were. But when Jesus asked that question, "Who do you say that I am?" suddenly it all came clear to Peter. He saw it in a flash, in a sudden grasp of truth, and he said, "Why, you're the Christ, the Son of the living God." The Lord Jesus said to him, "Peter, blessed are you!" (because God had done something for him.) He hadn't learned that by flesh and blood. He hadn't reasoned it out. He hadn't amassed all the evidence and come to a reasonable conclusion as to what who Christ was—but the Father had revealed it to him. That is the anointing, the teaching of the Spirit

# Chapter 21

# The Weapon of Mixture

*"Another parable He put forth to them, saying: 'The kingdom of heaven is like a man who sowed good seed in his field; but while men slept, his enemy came and sowed tares among the wheat and went his way. But when the grain had sprouted and produced a crop, then the tares also appeared. So the servants of the owner came and said to him, "Sir, did you not sow good seed in your field? How then does it have tares?" He said to them, "An enemy has done this." The servants said to him, "Do you want us then to go and gather them up?" But he said, "No, lest while you gather up the tares you also uproot the wheat with them. Let both grow together until the harvest, and at the time of harvest I will say to the reapers, 'First gather together the tares and bind them in bundles to burn them, but gather the wheat into my barn'"'"*
(Matthew 13:24–30).

When we use the term mixture we are emphasizing impurities in our walk with God. Satan suggests compromises. Satan will always come and suggest that we are giving 99% of our life to God; just 1% of sin won't hurt. This is compromise. We are living in such times that if there is anything that is hurting the Church of

Jesus Christ it is mixture in the lives of His people. Our heart, our eyes, and our walk needs to be 100% pure.

Satan consistently suggests that watching a two–hour, R-rated movie won't hurt. He'll say things like, "After all you've been pressing hard after God the whole week, two hours won't hurt." He's manipulating you to allow mixture in your life. We cannot compromise. We need to stand firm in our covenant with God. I have seen people compromise in their finances and have never tithed and wonder how come the blessing of the Lord is far from them. I have seen people compromise in their commitment to the local church and wonder why they are not being fruitful in their family.

When God calls us to walk with Him He expects 100% obedience, nothing less. When we give anything less than 100%, we insult the sacrifice of God made to redeem us. We need to understand it is impossible to give a 100%, but God has given His grace, His Holy Spirit, His Word, and all promises to help us to give our 100% pure walk for His glory. When God called Abraham, He told him to leave his country, his father's house, and his family. Abraham allowed a little mixture. He didn't obey completely. He compromised and took along Lot who was not part of the deal. Later, when we read Genesis 13–14, we find that Abraham had some problems with Lot. In another example, when Saul was told to go and kill all of the people of the Agagites, he compromised. At another time, he didn't wait for the prophet Samuel to come and offer the sacrifice. He took things into his own hands, mixing in his own plans. God removed His hand from Saul's life. I want you to understand that God will not tolerate mixture. Let's give God our best for He gave us His very Best, even Jesus Christ.

# Chapter 22

# The Weapon of Affliction

*"'So ought not this woman, being a daughter of Abraham, whom Satan has bound—think of it—for eighteen years, be loosed from this bond on the Sabbath?'"* (Luke 13:16).

*"And lest I should be exalted above measure by the abundance of the revelations, a thorn in the flesh was given to me, a messenger of Satan to buffet me, lest I be exalted above measure"* (2 Corinthians 12:7).

As I said earlier, we are spiritual beings. This means that we are not just bodies. We do not only exist in a physical dimension. We also have a spiritual dimension. Man, indeed is a tri-part being, having spirit, soul, and body. The Apostle Paul said in 1 Thessalonians 5:23, "Now may the God of peace Himself sanctify you completely; and may your whole spirit, soul, and body be preserved blameless at the coming of our Lord Jesus Christ." Since we are a tri-part being, Satan also seeks to afflict us in all three parts.

## Our Spirit
The Scriptures inform us that our spirit can be:
- Broken—"A wholesome tongue is a tree of life, but perverseness in it breaks the spirit" (Proverbs 15:4). "A merry heart

makes a cheerful countenance, but a broken spirit dries the bones" (Proverbs 15:12). "The spirit of a man will sustain him in sickness, but who can bear a broken spirit?" (Proverbs 18:14).

- Dried out—"A merry heart does good, like medicine, but a broken spirit dries the bones" (Proverbs 17:22).
- Hopeless—"The hand of the LORD came upon me and brought me out in the Spirit of the LORD, and set me down in the midst of the valley; and it was full of dry bones. Then He caused me to pass by them all around, and behold, there were many in the open valley; and indeed they were very dry" (Ezekiel 37:1–2).
- Sick—"Hope deferred makes the heart sick" (Proverbs 13:12).
- Defenseless—"Whoever has no rule over his own spirit is like a city broken down, without walls" (Proverbs 25:28).

## Our Soul

Remember that our soul is made up of memory, imaginations, emotions, will, and intellect. Satan may suddenly cause memory loss. He may attempt to infiltrate our imagination with wrong images. Our emotions can be controlled by evil spirits when we allow bitterness, hurt, etc. to rule our lives. Our will power and intellect can get so negatively affected by him and his cohorts that we become confused and unable to make right decisions.

## Our Body

Keep in mind that Satan is the source of sickness but not always the channel. Many times when it's cold weather we don't take care of our body by wearing proper clothes and get sick. So the channels are many but the source of sickness for the body is Satan. He will afflict the body with all kinds of sicknesses.

In all these things remember our God is *Jehovah Rapha*, the Lord who heals (Exodus 15:26). Here are four principles in knowing God intimately as *Jehovah Rapha*.

## Heed His Voice

This first point means that we have to be led by the Spirit. In Exodus 15:26, God said to Moses, "'If you diligently heed the voice of the LORD your God and do what is right in His sight, give ear to His commandments and keep all His statutes, I will put none of the diseases on you which I have brought on the Egyptians. For I am the LORD who heals you.'" Hearing the Holy Spirit is a part of knowing the healing powers of *Jehovah Rapha*.

We know that even in prosperity, you can be doing all the right things, but if the Spirit does not lead you and you are in the wrong place at the wrong time, you won't get your providential supply from God. It is important to be doing the right thing and to be in the right place at the right time for the supply of our God to come into our lives. Healing operates in a similar way.

The leading of the Holy Spirit and the Word of God work together. You can keep on uttering God's Biblical promises for healing all the time, but if the Holy Spirit tells you to cut back on eating certain foods or certain amounts of food, and you are not listening to the Holy Spirit, you can still be sick. If the Holy Spirit tells you not to nurse resentment and grudges against someone, and you don't listen, you can still suffer bodily. You are just trying to keep the letter of the Lord without following the Spirit.

## Do What is Right

There are two words in this principle that gives us revelation "do" and "right" or to use one word, "righteousness." Righteousness and healing are twins. They go together. There is no point trying to get healed if you are living in sin. God told Moses the people had to do what was right in His eyes. A lot of people don't get healing because they still want to live in sin. Remember that it is sin that brought sicknesses, disease, and death in the first place. Not all sicknesses are caused by personal sin, but some are. And some could just be sin of omission rather than sin of commission.

## Obey His Commandments

The commandments mentioned in Exodus 15:26 refer to God's Word. Proverbs 4:20–22 says, "My son, give attention to my words;

incline your ear to my sayings. Do not let them depart from your eyes; keep them in the midst of your heart; for they are life to those who find them, and health to all their flesh." Obeying God's commandments is life and health to us.

One of the commandments is to love our neighbours. When we harbour unforgiveness or when we envy or covet our neighbours possessions, we are not obeying God's command. If we are guilty of not loving our neighbours, we don't need to be prayed for healing; we just need to forgive and love.

## Keep all God's Statutes

The fourth principle is following the pattern or statutes of Scripture for the healing from God. For example, when you are sick, the Bible says call the elders and let them anoint you with oil and the prayer of faith shall heal the sick. When you follow the statutes, the healing of *Jehovah Rapha* will be manifested. In your prayer, begin to hallow the name of *Jehovah Rapha* and follow the principles associated with the name.

# Chapter 23

# The Weapon of Fear

_"For God hath not given us the spirit of fear, but of power and of love and of a sound mind"_ (2 Timothy 1:7).

Fear is no small subject. It is mentioned in the Bible over 600 times. Over 366 times, the phrase, "fear not," is mentioned—one for each day of the year. There is a healthy fear—the fear of God—and satanic fear.

The spirit of fear is one of Satan's prime weapons. Whether or not it takes the form of insecurity, anxiety, worry, preoccupation with problems, or whatever, it is still fear. Many people have a lot of unhealthy fear in their lives. People suffer from the fear of death, fear of darkness, fear of being alone, fear of loneliness, fear of rejection, fear of heights. Continuing to live in fear like this allows Satan an open door into the lives of people. Paul warns Timothy that God has not given us the spirit of fear but of power, love, and a sound mind.

Fear is a spirit. Fear leads us to sin. Fear can cause sickness in the soul and body of a person. Fear brings confusion. Fear causes us to hide from God. Fear causes us to flee from the promise and place of God. The great revivalist, John Wesley wrote, "I have never known more than fifteen minutes of anxiety or fear. Whenever, I feel fearful emotions overtaking me, I just close my eyes and thank God that He is still on the throne reigning over everything, and I take comfort in His control over all the affairs of my life."

Among many fears, there are seven dominant ones we have to overcome in our spiritual growth.

## Fear of Rejection

This is a fear of being made a fool or failing in the presence of others. Such fear usually begins in childhood and continue throughout the life of the individual. Maybe the criticism of parents, brothers, or even school friends caused the fear. After a while, when it is not dealt with, it becomes a spirit of fear of rejection. The fear is cast out by love. "There is no fear in love; but perfect love casts out fear, because fear involves torment. But he who fears has not been made perfect in love" (1 John 4:18).

## Fear of Change

We hate change, yet continuously we face it. Our physical bodies change. Friends change. Jobs change. Families change. This fear is removed from our life by pursuing God-given vision. Vision will strengthen us to embrace change. Psalms 55:22 tells us to "Cast your cares on the LORD and he will sustain you; he will never let the righteous fall" (NIV).

## Fear of Lack

It has been said that people want money because of the fear of lack because people don't want to be without food on their tables or clothes on their backs. Anytime the weatherman announces bad weather that could affect our communities for one or two days, all the grocery stores are empty of bread, milk, and other staples. We have to remember that there might be a famine, but we who are in obedience to God's law will be provided for (Philippians 4:19).

## Fear of Betrayal

Every divorce is born in betrayal. Every act of gossip is an act of betrayal. We have to overcome this by seeing the faithfulness of Jesus to us. Our security has to come in our relationship with Jesus.

And any relationship we have must be based on our trust in the Father and not in man.

As we follow Christ's example, we are bound to experience betrayal. After all, that's what He faced before He faced the cross. We just need to put our trust in Him who will never leave us, forsake us, or betray us.

## Fear of the Unknown

This is the reason in the present time that so many are turning to horoscopes, to play Ouija boards, and consult palm readers. This type of fear is dealt with by knowing God's purposes for our lives. He is a faithful God who declares the end from the beginning. The more we spend time in God's Word, the more you will be secure for your future. The Bible says in Jeremiah 29:11 that the plans that God has for you are to create a future and a hope. Rejoice in a known future through Jesus Christ.

## Fear of Failure

Many times we fail before we succeed. History is made up of men and women who have Ph.D.'s in failure, yet they overcame through perseverance. Perseverance will knock out the fear of failure. This kind of persevering power can only be received as you maintain your daily walk with God. "'Fear thou not; for I am with thee: be not dismayed; for I am thy God: I will strengthen thee; yea, I will help thee; yea, I will uphold thee with the right hand of my righteousness" (Isaiah 41:10, KJV).

## Fear of Death

A person whose sins have been forgiven by Jesus Christ and is walking in the light of God's Word need not fear death. For a believer, death is only a door to everlasting life in the manifest presence of Jesus. For the unbeliever, it is a door of everlasting life in torment. We do not need to fear death because Jesus has won for us life eternal!

# Chapter 24

# The Weapon of Enforcing Rebellion

We have talked a little about rebellion in our chapter on how the conflict began. The Bible tells us the rebellion is as the sin of witchcraft (1 Samuel 15:23). The essence of rebellion is the rejection of the righteous, legal, legitimate government of God in one's life. In the Garden of Eden, Adam rejected God's legitimate authority and thus became a rebel. Even in today's day, we see the working of rebellion in many forms including gay marriages, division of churches, etc. Remember a rebellious person is a selfish person. He seeks to please himself without the help of God. The Bible bids us to honor God. When we honor God's set authority, we honor Him. When we dishonor God's set authority, we dishonor Him.

In the rebellion family, there are several members that operate together. They are control, manipulation, domination, and stubbornness. These work hand in hand to enforce rebellion. Jezebel in 1 Kings is a perfect example of a person who has this spirit of the world operating to control, manipulate, and dominate the lives of others. We need to bind and cast out this Jezebel spirit.

## Control

We find unhealthy control in husband-wife relationships, parent-child relationships, pastor-congregation relationships, etc. We seek to direct how people should do this and that according to our pleasure and not really according to God's Word. When we attempt to control others, we are guilty of working with our enemy.

## Manipulate

This happens so often in families. Haven't you seen a mother and child shopping? Suddenly a child picks up some kind of expensive treat and begs his mother for it. The mother says no, and suddenly the child starts crying out loud to make a show. The mother may feel embarrassed and, consequently, give the child whatever he wants to keep the noise down. That is manipulation. Such manipulation can grow and abound if left unchecked.

## Dominate

The Genesis commandment was for man to dominate everything on earth except people. Satan tries to dominate people. We see so much of this in work places.

## Stubbornness

It is selfishness, pure and simple. A great antidote for rebellion is full submission to the work of the cross in our lives. We have to die daily to our selfish way and obey the ways of God. We can only experience the peace and satisfaction of God when we are in line with God's ways.

# PART V

# The Believer's Weapons

# Chapter 25

# Spiritual Weapons

*"For though we walk in the flesh, we do not war according to the flesh. For the **weapons of our warfare** are not carnal but **mighty in God** for pulling down strongholds, casting down arguments and every high thing that exalts itself against the knowledge of God, bringing every thought into captivity to the obedience of Christ, and being ready to punish all disobedience when your obedience is fulfilled"* (2 Corinthians 10:3–6, emphasis added).

There are two branches of warfare in the natural world: offensive and defensive. The Bible also teaches both defensive and offensive spiritual strategies. You must learn to fight both defensively and offensively. The only other option is desertion, which is unacceptable. Many say among the armors listed in Ephesians 6 the only offensive armor is the sword of the Spirit. In my opinion, all the armors are offensive and defensive. You can take the helmet and use it as an offensive weapon; you can take the shield and use it as an offensive weapon, as you can every other piece of armor.

There is one thing in common about offensive and defensive spiritual warfare. Both involve personal action by the believer. In natural warfare, unused weapons do not inflict causalities on the enemy, neither do they win wars. The same is true in the spirit world.

Your spiritual weapons are affected by your will to use them. It is true that God empowers for battle, but you have a personal responsibility in both defensive and offensive spiritual strategies. In Old Testament battles, the Lord fought for and with His people, Israel. But first, they had to position themselves on the battlefield.

The story of Elisha in 2 Kings 13:14–19 gives us some spiritual insight regarding the believer and his weapons.

> Elisha had become sick with the illness of which he would die. Then Joash the king of Israel came down to him, and wept over his face, and said, "O my father, my father, the chariots of Israel and their horsemen!" And Elisha said to him, "Take a bow and some arrows." So he took himself a bow and some arrows. Then he said to the king of Israel, "Put your hand on the bow." So he put his hand on it, and Elisha put his hands on the king's hands. And he said, "Open the east window"; and he opened it. Then Elisha said, "Shoot"; and he shot. And he said, "The arrow of the Lord's deliverance and the arrow of deliverance from Syria; for you must strike the Syrians at Aphek till you have destroyed them." Then he said, "Take the arrows"; so he took them. And he said to the king of Israel, "Strike the ground"; so he struck three times, and stopped. And the man of God was angry with him, and said, "You should have struck five or six times; then you would have struck Syria till you had destroyed it! But now you will strike Syria only three times."

## Take Initiative to Fight

Elisha told King Joash, "'Take up the bow and arrows.'" Paul said, "Take the sword of the Spirit" and declare war. By taking up your offensive and defensive weapons, you are taking responsibility. You must take the initiative to fight!

## Put Your Hands on the Weapons

Elisha told the king to put his hands upon the bow, and then Elisha laid his hands upon the king's hands. The strategy for victory is your hand upon the weapon and God's hand over yours. Putting your hands on the weapons speaks of our action—that your decision is followed with actions. So many people have made decisions to do things, but they are never accomplished because they never followed their decisions with actions.

## Open the Window

Israel's foe was to the east, so Elisha told the king to open the window eastward. We must open the window to face our enemy. God wants you to open up the "windows" of every area of our lives to expose the failure, defeat, and bondage of the enemy. In warfare, there should be a target, and the way must be cleared to hit your target.

## Shoot

Elisha told the king, "'Shoot,'" and the king shot. Then Elisha said, "'The Lord's arrow of victory over Syria.'" The open window is not enough. The weapon in your hand is not sufficient. Even God's hand upon your hand will not win the battle. You must follow the command of the Lord of Host to SHOOT!

## Know Your Objective

Elisha told the King to take the arrows and hit them upon the ground as a symbol of his victory over Syria. The king did so, but he only struck the ground three times. Elisha told him that because he limited God by hitting the ground only three times, his military victory would be limited. This happened because the king did not understand the objective of warfare. Elisha had said the Lord wanted to totally consume the enemy (verse 17). By striking the ground only three times, the king settled for only partial victory. The Lord's objective for you is total victory in every area of your life and ministry. If you fail to understand this objective, then your victory will be limited. Don't limit God.

## You are Already a Champion

The Battlefield does not make you a champion; it only proves you stepped out on the battlefield as a champion. Racecar drivers are champions before they get behind the wheel. When the race is finished, it only proves that they got in the car as champions. What happened between Elisha and King Joash in the secret chamber that day determined the outcome of the battle with Syria. It is what happens in your secret chamber with the Lord that determines your victories in the actual battles of life.

So let's use our weapons and take charge and extend the Kingdom of God. The Bible tells us that as believers we have many weapons to cancel the assignments of Satan, to quench his power, and walk in the joy of the Lord. Out of the many weapons like the weapons of praise, weapon of thanksgiving, weapon of worship, weapon of prayer, we will only talk about seven weapons. You can see my first book for discussion of the weapons we do not address here.

# Chapter 26

# The Weapon of Repentance

*"'Repent therefore and be converted, that your sins may be blotted out, so that times of refreshing may come from the presence of the Lord'"* (Acts 3:19).

Jesus referred to the believer as both light and salt. But His descriptions of the believer came with warnings. Salt can lose its savor, and the light can be hidden under a bushel. Many have lost their savor and their position in the plan of God because of sin. That's why many in the Kingdom of God are busy but ineffective; but praise God for the ability to repent. Repentance is given for our benefit that we can turn back to the place and position God has for us. That repentance is also a weapon that destroys the enemy's hold over our lives.

Many define repentance as a change of mind, change of thoughts, a total turnaround in life. I simply say, "Repentance is making necessary changes—whether in mind, body, spirit, attitude, or whatever other area—to be in the position God has for us and receive the power to fulfill our God-given assignment." Repentance is an ongoing process. It's not a one-time event that happens at conversion. Repentance is a response to the revelation we have had. Repentance doesn't just come by looking inward and seeing sin. People that are living in sin really don't care to look inward and see their sin. The conviction can only come through the Holy Spirit. In Isaiah 6, Isaiah first had an upward vision of the glory of God, then conviction came on him so he could receive a revelation of the holiness of God, and his own unholy condition. This caused repentance to come in his life.

Many people want revival, but revival will not come unless there is repentance. Acts 3:19–21 reads, "'Repent therefore and be converted, that your sins may be blotted out, so that times of refreshing may come from the presence of the Lord, and that He may send Jesus Christ, who was preached to you before, whom heaven must receive until the times of restoration of all things, which God has spoken by the mouth of all His holy prophets since the world began.'" This tells us four things: repent and be converted so that times of refreshing, restoration, and the return of Christ may come.

A.W. Tozer said that there can be "no revival without reformation." The following is an excerpt from his writings:

> Unless we intend to reform, we may as well not pray. Unless praying men have the insight and faith to amend their whole way of life to conform to the New Testament pattern, there can be no revival....God is not interested in increasing church attendance unless those who attend amend their ways and begin to live holy lives. Prayer for revival will prevail when it is accompanied by radical amendment of life; not before. All night prayer meetings that are not preceded by practical repentance may actually be displeasing to God.

So as we continue to talk about repentance, we need to identify it on three different levels—namely, individual repentance, corporate repentance, and identification repentance. These three are highlighted throughout the Scriptures.

## Individual Repentance

John warns us in his first epistle:

> If we say that we have fellowship with Him, and walk in darkness, we lie and do not practice the truth. But if we walk

in the light as He is in the light, we have fellowship with one another, and the blood of Jesus Christ His Son cleanses us from all sin. If we say that we have no sin, we deceive ourselves, and the truth is not in us. If we confess our sins, He is faithful and just to forgive us our sins and to cleanse us from all unrighteousness (1:6–9).

As I said before, repentance is making any necessary change whether in mind, body, spirit, attitude or whatever other area so as to be in the position God has for us and receive the power to fulfill our God-given assignment. We want to ensure we are walking in the light and not merely deceiving ourselves. Psalm 24 helps us to see what areas need to be looked in order to do this—"Who may ascend into the hill of the LORD? Or who may stand in His holy place? He who has clean hands and a pure heart, who has not lifted up his soul to an idol, nor sworn deceitfully" (3–4).

We see in Psalm 24 four important things:

- Clean hands—these speak of our actions;
- A pure heart—this speaks about our attitudes and motives;
- A soul not lifted up to an idol—this speaks about our loves and affections; and
- Not having sworn deceitfully—speaks about our mouths or tongues.

These areas are pointed out so that we can look at each one of them and ask the Holy Spirit to help us see things that are hindrances so that we can repent and get back to the place we belong. It is said of Charles Finney that he prepared a list of possible sins for people to check their lives against. But we can look the areas mentioned above to see if there be any wicked way in us. As Finney said, "General confession of Sin will never do. Your sins were committed one by one, and they should be reviewed and repented of one by one."

Another man wonderfully used by God was Evan Robert. He is the name we associate with the Welsh Revival of the early 1900's. He said:

Is there any sin in your past that you have not confessed to God? On your knees at once! Your past must be put away and your self cleansed. Is there anything in your life that is doubtful—anything that you cannot decide whether it is good or evil? Away with it! There must not be a cloud between you and God. Have you forgiven everybody, EVERYBODY? If not, don't expect forgiveness for your own sins. You won't get it! Do what the Spirit prompts you to do. Obedience—prompt, implicit, unquestioning obedience to the Spirit. You must confess Christ publicly.

## Corporate Repentance

Jesus told the church at Ephesus in Revelation 2:4–5, "'Nevertheless I have this against you, that you have left your first love. Remember therefore from where you have fallen; repent and do the first works, or else I will come to you quickly and remove your lampstand from its place—unless you repent.'" Jesus called this church and four others listed in chapters two and three of Revelation to repent, actually to corporate repentance.

Jesus is building His Church. And as He said through Paul to the Ephesians He's desirous to have a glorious church without spot or wrinkle (5:26–27). His Church, then, will have to ensure her right-standing through sincere repentance.

I see three purposes for the Church. Her first purpose is her ministry to the Lord, her second is the ministry of her Body to one another, and the third is her ministry to the world. In light of these purposes, we as members of the Church need to evaluate if there is anyway in which we have fallen short of fulfilling our purposes.

When it comes to our ministry to the Lord, how is our passion for Him? Are there any distractions? Do we still have the fear of the Lord? Do we honor Him as we ought?

How about our ministry to one another in the Body of Christ? Are we allowing our gifts and anointing to gel together and work with one another? Are we fulfilling our vision? Is there unity? Are we in submission to the authority, or do we have a rebellious, independent attitude? Are we faithful in assembling together?

And lastly how is our ministry to the world going? Are we using every method possible to show and share the love of Christ? Are people being born into the Kingdom of God? Are we more concerned about building than we are about people? Are we committed to world missions?

# Identification Repentance

What is identification repentance? Identification repentance is when we join ourselves to a group of people, like a church, city, state, or a nation and confess our and their sins. This was very common in the Scriptures. Nehemiah, for example, when he heard about the news of the city of Jerusalem, displayed identification repentance. He confessed his own sin and then included himself as part of the sins of their forefathers and the sins of their nation or people group (1:4–9). Remember he said, "'*We* have sinned'" and not "*They* have sinned." Identification repentance is what Jesus did for us. He identified with us. He joined with us. He became sin for us and brought about reconciliation.

An important verse that addresses this type of repentance is found in 2 Chronicles 7:14—"'if My people who are called by My name will humble themselves, and pray and seek My face, and turn from their wicked ways, then I will hear from heaven, and will forgive their sin and heal their land.'" Here are the four parts to identification repentance:

- Humility. This comes through brokenness.
- Prayer. We understand that only God can give us the power to forsake sin, and we are totally dependent upon Him.
- Seeking God. This speaks of intimacy, of having a desire to reconcile with God.
- Forsaking sin. God partners with us and cleanses us step by step.

We need to confess our sin and repent, and God will hear us and break the strongholds of Satan over our cities, states, and nations. Again let me make it clear, Satan has gained territory because of the sins of people. Sin gives him an open door to expand his territory.

We have to break through barriers, walls, hedges that Satan has built around things that have been snatched from us because of our sin. Like Jericho, the walls of our cities have been shut tightly, but by the marching of the people of God, by shouts of praise, and unity, those barriers can be broken down and the land claimed for God. In the same manner, we need to seek the face of God for keys to unlock our churches, our neighborhoods, our cities, our states, and our nations. We need to break the barrier and claim the people, resources, land, etc. for the Kingdom of God.

Many people live in a city and no clue as to its history. It would be of great help in prayer and repentance to do some research and find out the history of it. We need to ask questions like:

- What is the population?
- How many cultures or people groups are there?
- What percentage of people attends church?
- How many are living in poverty?
- What are any major highlights?
- What were the religious practices?
- What influences the government?
- Has the city been involved in any wars, fights, national stands?
- What is the meaning of the name of the city?
- Does it have a nickname? Why does it have that name?
- Who were the founders?
- Has the city ever faced any traumatic experiences like an earthquake or flood, when did it happen?

The above things can help us pray, identify areas of sin or needs for prayer, and provoke us to repent. Someone recently asked me whether I believe in the concept of spiritual mapping. My response was that anything that helps us get aware of the battle we are facing in our neighborhoods, cities, etc. is always helpful. These things are merely tools to get the job done. The information we collect are only tools to help us; all the while our focus should be on Jesus and His resources to get the job done. Always remember the insight we gain should not only be natural things like history, demographics, but we need to hear from the Holy Spirit. The Holy Spirit is the best Person to uncover the root of things. The reason for Spiritual Mapping is only to prepare for invasion of God's purpose. It's not there to compare our strength with the enemy's strength. There is no comparison. Abraham was told to survey the land which he was to possess. Jesus overlooked the city of Jerusalem and surveyed its anguish. So we know that it's a Biblical principle to survey the city, but remember that it's only a tool.

# Chapter 27

# The Weapon of the Blood of Jesus

*"'And they overcame him [Satan] by the blood of the Lamb...'"* (Revelation 12:11).

Oone of the greatest weapons we have available is the weapon of the blood of Jesus. Nowadays, we don't hear a lot about the blood of Jesus. But I want to tell you one of the most important topics, subjects, theme, power, in the Scriptures is the blood of Jesus.

The blood of Jesus is a powerful weapon against guilt and shame. All of us are troubled by recurring problems of this kind or another. Many people think that guilty feelings are really the voice of God, but sometimes they're deceived. It's one thing to sin and feel guilty; it's quite another to have not sinned and yet feel guilty. The devil uses guilt to frustrate and defeat us. We know that Satan is the accuser of the brethren. By accusation, he endeavors to produce guilt in our lives. When the Holy Spirit points out sin, He always points the way to Jesus for forgiveness and righteousness.

The Scriptures outline several benefits that we have received by the blood of Jesus like cleansing, forgiveness, righteousness, etc. But the question is how do we get the power of the blood applied to our lives? How is the shed blood of Jesus used as a weapon?

In Revelation 12, as we noted in the chapter on testimony, it says, "'They overcame him by the blood of the Lamb and by the word of their testimony'" (11). A simple way to say that is they overcome him (Satan) by testifying, proclaiming with their mouths what the Word of God says that the blood of Jesus had done for them.

In the Exodus 12, a beautiful analogy is given of how the blood works in our lives. Israel had been in bondage to Pharaoh for 400 years. So as Israel cried out for help, God sent Moses as a deliverer.

Moses went and asked Pharaoh to let the people of Israel go, yet Pharaoh's heart got hardened and would not let them go. So God began to send plagues to move the Egyptians to let His people go. The book of Exodus records ten plagues that were sent like hail, boils, etc. One among them was moving of the death angel throughout the land to take the life of every firstborn. The children of Israel were told to take a lamb, cut it, and allow its blood to be shed in a basin. Then, they were to take a hyssop, which was just a shrub of a tree, and apply the blood from the basin to the doorposts of their houses. When the death angel saw the blood, the angel passed over and didn't harm anyone in the house.

Here we see the power of the blood. In the same manner, Jesus' blood was not only shed on the cross of Calvary, but the Bible says that Jesus entered the Holy of Holies in the sanctuary of heaven and sprinkled that blood in a basin so that you and I can be accepted by the Father. But then how do we get the blood from that basin to our lives? Well, that's simple. We do this by using a hyssop. Only our hyssop is faith and confession. We have to have faith that the Word of God is true in its proclamation of the blood of Jesus, and then we have to confess with our mouths the power of that blood. So let's take a look at some of the benefits and apply that blood, using it as a weapon against the forces of Satan.

Below I ask that you read the Scriptures under each subheading and then say the confessions aloud.

## Redemption and Forgiveness

*"In Him we have redemption through His blood, the forgiveness of sins, according to the riches of His grace"* (Ephesians 1:7).

- **Confession.** According to Ephesians 1:7, by the blood of Jesus, I have been redeemed, which means that I was a slave of the kingdom of Satan, but I have been bought by the price of the blood. Now I belong to the Kingdom of Jesus Christ. I am no longer a slave of Satan but a son [or daughter] in the family of God.
- **Confession.** According to Ephesians 1:7, the blood of Jesus Christ has forgiven me from all my sins, and the power of sin has been broken in my life.

## Justification

*"Much more then, having now been justified by His blood, we shall be saved from wrath through Him"* (Romans 5:9).

- **Confession.** According to Romans 5:9, the blood of Jesus has justified me, which means I'm in right standing with God and His laws, just as if I had never sinned.

## Protection

*"For I will pass through the land of Egypt on that night, and will strike all the firstborn in the land of Egypt, both man and beast; and against all the gods of Egypt I will execute judgment: I am the LORD. Now the blood shall be a sign for you on the houses where you are. And when I see the blood, I will pass over you; and the plague shall not be on you to destroy you when I strike the land of Egypt"* (Exodus 12:12–13).

When we read the above verse, it appears that God is the one who does the smiting upon the firstborn. But when we read verse 23, we find out that there are two people involved—God and the destroyer. """For the LORD will pass through to strike the Egyptians; and when he sees the blood on the lintel and on the two doorposts, the LORD will pass [as a guard] over the door and not allow the destroyer to come in unto your houses to strike you.""" Notice that God guards over the blood-sprinkled door and does not permit the destroyer to come in the house to smite the firstborn. So it is with us. We need to plead the blood of Jesus over our lives, and God Himself will stand guard and not allow the devil to touch us. Every night before I go to sleep, I plead the blood of Jesus over every door, window, sleeping place, and every person of the house—that no tricks of the enemy, no assignments of Satan, no bad dreams, evil presence shall penetrate.

- **Confession.** According to Exodus 12, as the blood was applied to the house, I plead the blood of Jesus over my life and my possessions. Nothing of the enemy shall penetrate me or what's mine. I am protected by God himself. My security comes only from Him.

## Sanctification

*"Therefore Jesus also, that He might sanctify the people with His own blood"* (Hebrews 13:12).

What does sanctification mean? It means that you are set apart, consecrated, Holy unto God. You might not feel holy. As a matter of fact, the devil will try to tell you a lot of things, but know this: Jesus by His own blood has made you Holy and calls you Holy.

- **Confession:** According to Hebrews 13:12, I am sanctified, set apart for God, consecrated for His service, and made Holy unto God. My body is the temple of the Holy Spirit, not by my works, but by the blood of Jesus Christ my Savior.

## Cleansing

*"If we say that we have fellowship with Him, and walk in darkness, we lie and do not practice the truth. But if we walk*

*in the light as He is in the light, we have fellowship with one another, and the blood of Jesus Christ His Son cleanses us from all sin. If we say that we have no sin, we deceive ourselves, and the truth is not in us. If we confess our sins, He is faithful and just to forgive us our sins and to cleanse us from all unrighteousness"* (1 John 1:6–9).

- **Confession.** According to 1 John 1:6–9, as I walk in the light with Jesus the blood of Jesus continually cleanses me and causes me to have fellowship with God and others. Even if I commit sin, when I confess it, it's forgiven. Satan has no place in me. I rebuke his power over my life in Jesus' name.

# The Blood Speaks

*"To Jesus the Mediator of the new covenant, and to the blood of sprinkling that speaks better things than that of Abel"* (Hebrews 12:24).

- **Confession.** The blood of Jesus that is sprinkled in the sanctuary of heaven is speaking on my behalf.

# Overcoming Life Power

*"For the life of the flesh is in the blood..."* (Leviticus 17:11).

*"And they overcame him by the blood of the Lamb..."* (Revelation 12:11).

- **Confession.** The blood of Jesus has overcoming power in my life. There is life in the blood of Jesus.

# Communing Privilege

*"The cup of blessing which we bless, is it not the communion of the blood of Christ? The bread which we break, is*

*it not the communion of the body of Christ"* (1 Corinthians 10:16).

- **Confession.** According to 1 Corinthians 10:16, the blood of Jesus gives me the privilege of fellowshipping with other believers and sharing in the work of the kingdom.

## Peace

*"And by Him to reconcile all things to Himself, by Him, whether things on earth or things in heaven, having made peace through the blood of His cross"* (Colossians 1:20).

- **Confession.** According to the Colossians 1:20, the blood of Jesus produced peace in my life. Satan has no right to torment, harass, or condemn me. I have the peace of God. My relationship with God is secure.

## Access

*"Therefore, brethren, having boldness to enter the Holiest by the blood of Jesus"* (Hebrews 10:19).

- **Confession.** According to Hebrews 10:19, I am permitted to enter the presence of God boldly to obtain grace and mercy. I have no excuse for not fellowshipping with God, for Jesus has made the way and given me access.

# Chapter 28

# The Weapon of the Name of Jesus

*"All nations surrounded me, but in the **name of the** LORD *I will destroy them. They surrounded me, yes, they surrounded me; but in the **name of the** LORD *I will destroy them. They surrounded me like bees; they were quenched like a fire of thorns; for in the **name of the** LORD *I will destroy them"* (Psalm 118:10–12, emphasis added).

There is power in the name of Jesus. The devil trembles at the name of Jesus. Demons tremble at the name of Jesus. The Bible says everything in heaven, on earth, and below has to bow in submission to the name of Jesus. When Peter and John were walking to the temple in Acts 3, the lame man who was at the gate was begging for alms. Peter spoke up and said, "'Silver and gold I do not have, but what I do have I give you: In the name of Jesus Christ of Nazareth, rise up and walk'" (6). The lame man was healed with the weapon of the name of Jesus.

In Acts 4:7, when Peter and John were called in by Annas and Caiaphas, the high priests, they asked them a question: "'By what power or by what name, have ye done this?'" Somehow they knew that a name had brought healing to the lame man, and they wanted to know more about how and why they were using that name. The leaders commanded Peter and John not to speak or teach in the name of Jesus (18). Please understand there is so much power in the name of Jesus that even people who are not living right are convicted of their condition without anyone ever pointing it out to them.

Later on in that same chapter of Acts, Peter and John returned to their companions and told them their report. Their response was to cry out to God together asking, "'Now, Lord, look on their threats, and grant to Your servants that with all boldness they may speak Your word, by stretching out Your hand to heal, and that signs and wonders may be done through the name of Your holy Servant Jesus'"(29–30). All of these wonderful things they asked of God, knowing they could be done only in the name of Jesus.

James 5:14 affirms the power of the name of the Lord for healing, "Is anyone among you sick? Let him call for the elders of the church, and let them pray over him, anointing him with oil in the name of the Lord."

For more study on the subject of the name of Jesus, see my first book, *Believer's Mandate—Foundation for Abundant Life*.

# Chapter 29

# The Weapon of Personal Testimony

*"And they overcame him by the blood of the Lamb and by the word of their testimony..."* (Revelation 12:11, emphasis added).

The weapon of personal testimony is a weapon which is not used much by a believer, yet it is one of the most powerful weapons available to us. Revelation 12:11 says, "'They overcame him [Satan] by the blood of the Lamb and by the word of their testimony.'" So your personal testimony has overcoming power. Testimony is simply testifying what God has done. It's being a witness of God's power. It is proclaiming that what God did for me, He will do for you. It's voicing the power of God.

Everyone one of us has a testimony, but the question is have we ever opened our mouths and testified of the blessing of God. We have been healed or blessed with a car, with a house, with a family, and with clothes on our back, but do we ever testify about it? When you testify about God's provision, it seals your miracle. When God has blessed you, and you don't testify, you leave the door open for

Satan to rob you of your blessing. As soon as you testify, you bring glory to God, and God protects your blessing.

Giving a personal testimony is a great way to communicate the love of Jesus. You can tell people how you were sick, then you believed God's Word in regards to healing, and next you got healed. A person will believe you. The Holy Spirit will use that as an entrance into that person's life. I heard one preacher says, "A man with an argument is never at the mercy of a man with an experience."

The word of testimony also helps you to build faith and believe God for greater things. I always tell people that, when David was in front of Saul and wanted to go kill Goliath, David encouraged himself. He said, "Thy servant had killed a lion, thy servant had killed a bear so what is this Philistine before me; the Lord will deliver him also." David was giving a word of testimony regarding the power of God which was building and encouraging him. In the same manner, when we are holding healing meetings, we ask people who have sicknesses that are death sentences if God has ever healed them of anything. No matter how great or how small the healing, just remembering the testimony helps to build their faith. Say to you yourself, "I had a fever, and I believed the Word of God and confessed it with my mouth and stood strong and the Lord healed me, so what is this cancer? This will be healed also." Now that's the power of testimony. You are using it as a weapon against the tricks of Satan.

David wrote, "I will bless the LORD at all times; His praise shall continually be in my mouth" (Psalm 34:1). Here David is talking about praising God through testifying what He has done. One of the greatest problems with believers is that we FORGET the benefits we have received. Psalm 103:2 says, "Bless the LORD, O my soul, and forget not all His benefits." Testifying of God's work in our lives helps us remember and rehearse God's deliverance so that we can move forward in the things God has for us.

The writer of Hebrews encourages us to recall what God has done and use it as power to go forward.

But recall the former days in which, after you were illuminated, you endured a great struggle with sufferings: partly while you were made a spectacle both by reproaches and tribulations, and partly while you became companions of those who were so treated; for you had compassion on me in my chains, and joyfully accepted the plundering of your goods, knowing that you have a better and an enduring possession for yourselves in heaven. Therefore do not cast away your confidence, which has great reward. For you have need of endurance, so that after you have done the will of God, you may receive the promise (10:32–36).

In the Scripture passage above, the writer is not telling us to dwell on the glory days of the past. Recalling what God has done in the past is testifying of God's work in our lives. Testifying also cancels out our giving up on things that God has called us to possess. Testifying helps us persevere and build strong faith.

The disciples consistently forgot the miracles Jesus did so every time they had a problem they were worried. One time Jesus multiplied the fishes and loaves, but soon the disciples forgot, and crisis came, and they were crying out to Jesus. Instead, they should have had faith that if Jesus was with them there was no problem. So Jesus rebuked them. You see that each time Jesus multiplied the bread, there were baskets left over for the disciples as a reminder of what God can do, but instead they failed to remember and rehearse what God did. They were spiritually blind. Your personal testimony has great power; it can help you see and expect God to give you a new testimony.

Asaph in Psalm 77 expresses a feeling that most of us have felt time and again. He's discouraged about what he's seeing and experiencing, but he knows how to get out of that kind of discouraging atmosphere. He begins to remember and rehearse God's work in his life. He said, "I will remember the works of the LORD; surely I will remember Your wonders of old. I will also meditate on all Your work, and talk of Your deeds" (11). He was encouraged by His own testimony.

# Chapter 30

# The Weapon of the Gifts
# of the Holy Spirit

—⟶

The Gifts of the Spirit are tools, not toys, given to accomplish the work of the Gospel. First Corinthians 12 outlines nine gifts of the Holy Spirit. Each gift is a weapon that assassinates the devices and works of Satan.

## Word of Knowledge

A word of knowledge is simply a portion of the knowledge of God for past, present, or future. It is not the complete knowledge, but a portion of it just for the time.

In Acts 5, the gift of a word of knowledge exposed the deception and lies of Satan that Ananias and Sapphira allowed to control their destinies. Peter knew Ananias lied and kept back a portion of the profits from selling his land. He told him, "You have not lied to men but to God" (4).

## Word of Wisdom

The word of wisdom is a portion of God's wisdom that helps us know the true nature of a situation and helps us solve a problem. Many times when we are faced with a problem we may not know what to do. Wisdom helps us to discern what the truth is and gives us right direction in decision-making. When Jesus was faced with the people asking the question of paying taxes, He operated in wisdom, and it eliminated any scheming of man or trickery of Satan.

## Discerning of Spirits

Discerning of spirits is a weapon that eliminates wrong spirits, motives, and attitudes that operate in people. People outwardly may seem Godly and seem like they are doing right, yet they may have a filthy spirit, filthy attitude, or filthy motives. This gift gets to the bottom of things.

## Faith

The gift of faith is a weapon that eliminates doubt, unbelief, and fear. When it rises in the hearts of believers, it's a powerful weapon against the wiles of the enemy. People who were just too afraid or hopeless to rise up in faith may suddenly be lifted above their circumstance, believing God for the impossible.

## Healings

The gift of healings is a weapon that eliminates sickness, disease, and infirmity. It defeats Satan's attempts to destroy the lives of people.

## Miracles

The gift of miracles is a weapon that brings breakthrough. When Moses and the people of Israel were standing at the Red Sea, Moses lifted his rod, and the sea parted, enabling the Israelites to walk on dry ground.

## Tongues

The gift of tongues is a weapon that quenches discouragement, pride, etc. Jude encourages us to build up our spirit man by praying in tongues.

## Interpretation

The gift of interpretation works hand in hand with the gift of tongues. You can interpret the utterances the Holy Spirit gives. Once you have spoken in tongues, or whether you are in a group and someone speaks in tongue, you can also interpret. All you have to do is to pray that you may interpret what has been said in tongues. First Corinthians 14:13, "Wherefore let him that speaketh in an unknown tongue pray that he may interpret" (KJV). This gift helps to us to understand spiritual things with our natural mind.

## Prophecy

The gift of prophecy is a weapon that exposes the secrets of the hearts of people and causes them to come to repentance and to the exaltation of Jesus. First Corinthians 14:24–25 tells us, "But if all prophesy, and an unbeliever or an uninformed person comes in, he is convinced by all, he is convicted by all. And thus the secrets of his heart are revealed; and so, falling down on his face, he will worship God and report that God is truly among you."

# Chapter 31

# The Weapon of Wisdom

*"There was a little city with few men in it; and a great king came against it, besieged it, and built great snares around it. Now there was found in it a poor wise man, and he by his wisdom delivered the city. Yet no one remembered that same poor man. Then I said: 'Wisdom is better than strength. Nevertheless the poor man's wisdom is despised, and his words are not heard. Words of the wise, spoken quietly, should be heard rather than the shout of a ruler of fools. Wisdom is better than weapons of war; but one sinner destroys much good'"* (Ecclesiastes 9:14–18).

*"Plans are established by counsel; by wise counsel wage war"* (Proverbs 20:18).

Spiritual wisdom is a weapon we can use against the forces of the enemy. The man in Ecclesiastes 9 brought about a great deliverance for his city by wisdom. Wisdom was a defensive plan for his city, and wisdom was the offensive plan for it, too. Spiritual wisdom is better than weapons of natural war. Without it, in fact, you and I cannot maintain our place of victory.

What then is wisdom? Wisdom is the discovery of the true nature of an issue. It understands how God's purpose is to be implemented.

When Solomon had a visitation of God in his life, and God asked him what he wanted, Solomon requested wisdom. Soon after that, two women who had recently given birth to children came before him for judgment. They appear before Solomon over a dispute regarding a child. One woman claims a certain child is hers, while the other claims the child is hers. We learn in the story that one woman awoke to find her child dead. She went to another woman and stole her baby to replace her own. These two women stood before Solomon, and this was where Solomon requested a sword to cut the infant in two so that both women could have part of the child. The one woman who was willing to give up her half in order to spare the child was the rightful mother of the child. Solomon gave her the child. You see wisdom exposed deception in that case.

Wisdom is essential to life. Many say, "I need my spouse to love me." The Bible would say to you that, "You need wisdom to be a good spouse first." Wisdom is an absolute. Everyone has a measure of wisdom in his life. Some have a lot of it, some little. But it doesn't matter how much you have, you need more.

Jesus commands us in Matthew 10:16 to be wise as serpents. Therefore, to walk in wisdom is not an option but a requirement. You have to choose wisdom. You either choose to be wise, or you choose to be foolish. If you choose foolishness, you are opening a door for destruction. When we walk in wisdom, it guarantees us counsel, safety, security, and the absence of the fear of evil. "They would have none of my counsel and despised my every rebuke. Therefore they shall eat the fruit of their own way, and be filled to the full with their own fancies. For the turning away of the simple will slay them, and the complacency of fools will destroy them; but whoever listens to me will dwell safely, And will be secure, without fear of evil" (Proverbs 1:30–33).

God alone is wise, and therefore, wisdom can only be obtained from Him (Romans 16:27). In 1 Corinthians 1:30, we read, "But of Him you are in Christ Jesus, who became for us wisdom from God—and righteousness and sanctification and redemption". So God is the source of wisdom. Jesus is the channel for us to receive wisdom, and the Holy Spirit is the helper who helps us apply the wisdom.

In the book of Job, we find that Job's three friends said that wisdom is gained several ways, of which none are correct. Eliphaz comes to Job and says that wisdom is gained by observing and experiencing life; as time goes on you become wise. Then Bildad comes along and says that wisdom is inherited. That means you are to learn everything that has been said about wisdom till now, and if you understand it, then you are a candidate to progress and get wisdom for today. Finally, Zophar comes along and says that you have to associate with those who are wise and learn from them because wisdom is for the few and not for everyone. All three of them were wrong. God alone is the source of wisdom.

## Two Kinds of Wisdom

The opposite of spiritual wisdom is natural wisdom. The Apostle James labels natural wisdom as earthly, sensual, and even demonic.

> Who is wise and understanding among you? Let him show by good conduct that his works are done in the meekness of wisdom. But if you have bitter envy and self-seeking in your hearts, do not boast and lie against the truth. This wisdom does not descend from above, but is earthly, sensual, and demonic. For where envy and self-seeking exist, confusion and every evil thing are there (James 3:13).

Since Natural Wisdom is earthly, sensual, and demonic, it is characterized by envy, bitterness, selfish ambition, confusion, and destruction. The natural wisdom is of the earth; it is temporary. Natural wisdom is not always in line with God's Word. Natural wisdom is also sensual. Sensual wisdom does not refer only to sensuality or sexuality (outside of God's parameters) but also to the realm of feelings. Sensual wisdom says do this or that if it feels good. If you feel good about it, then that's right for your life. Natural wisdom is also demonic in that you can choose something outside of the will and Word of God, leaving a door open for Satan to come in.

James 3:17, however, gives us seven characteristics of wisdom that is from above. "But the wisdom that is from above is first pure, then peaceable, gentle, willing to yield, full of mercy and good fruits, without partiality and without hypocrisy."

- **Spiritual wisdom is pure.** It has no mixture of the world in it. In India 24-karat gold is very common, but in western countries 18-karat is more common. Many people don't like 24-karat gold because it's considered closest to pure gold. The reason for this is that the more pure the gold is the more malleable and soft it is. It is easy to bend. So people like lesser karats with the mixture that hardens the gold. But spiritual wisdom cannot have any mixture, so it is soft and malleable. This is because God wants our lives to be malleable in His hands. He wants our hearts to be soft in His hands. He wants us to be malleable and molded more and more into His image. He is shaping our lives by His design.
- **Spiritual wisdom is peaceable.** Spiritual wisdom always produces peace in your life, in your relationships, and also in your walk with God. Spiritual wisdom never leads to adversarial relationships. It never leads to strife, arguing, competition, or confusion. Jesus said in Matthew 5:9, "'Blessed are the peacemakers, for they shall be called sons of God.'"
- **Spiritual wisdom is gentle.** Spiritual wisdom is not harsh, arrogant, or demeaning. Jesus was noted as the Lamb of God which symbolized His gentleness. Spiritual wisdom will always cause you to deal in gentleness.
- **Spiritual wisdom is willingness to yield.** Spiritual wisdom is not inflexible and unteachable. Spiritual wisdom doesn't fight for personal rights. Spiritual wisdom is the absence of pride. It always promotes unity and a spirit humility.
- **Spiritual wisdom is full of mercy and good fruits.** Spiritual wisdom is not callous, unmoved, and stubborn. It always seeks to walk in forgiveness. It always focuses on producing fruits that endure. It causes us to always stay attached to the vine—Jesus Christ.
- **Spiritual wisdom is without partiality.** Spiritual wisdom is available to people who simply ask for it. We have to know our authority as children of the King and know that God is no respecter of persons. When we chose to leave the kingdom

of darkness and join the Kingdom of Light, the cost was the same for each and every one of us—the blood of Jesus.

- **Spiritual wisdom is without hypocrisy.** It is transparent, honest, and reveals integrity. It never allows you to hide behind a mask and live in a world of imagination.

# Chapter 32

# The Weapon of Intercessory Prayer

*"Likewise the Spirit also helps in our weaknesses. For we do not know what we should pray for as we ought, but the Spirit Himself makes intercession for us with groanings which cannot be uttered. Now He who searches the hearts knows what the mind of the Spirit is, because He makes intercession for the saints according to the will of God"* (Romans 8:26–27).

*"Intercessory prayer is intensified praying which involves three special ingredients:* **identification** *of the intercessor with the one whom is interceded for;* **agony** *to feel the burden, the pain, the suffering, the need;* **authority***. This is the gained position of the intercessor, to speak with authority that sees results"* (Rees Howells).

Intercessory prayer or intercession, in simple language, is being a mediator between two parties through prayer. Intercession is not prayer, but Intercession is done through prayer. An intercessor is a person who fights, prays, and intervenes on behalf of others. He or she forgets his or her personal needs and focuses on those of others.

*Webster's Dictionary* defines to intercede as, "Latin intercede: inter-between; ado—to go; literally to pass between) to act between parties with a view to reconcile those who differ or contend; to plead in favor of another; to mediate."

Since the Bible was written in Greek and Hebrew, the Hebrew word for intercession is the *paga*. There are at least four different pictures painted to grasp the nature of this Greek word:

- To meet;
- To light upon (by chance) or to fall upon;
- To attack or to strike down;
- To lay upon, to bear, to lift, or to carry.

To meet simply means to have a meeting. Through intercessory prayer or intercession, we meet with God and ask Him to meet with the party for whom we are standing on behalf. Understand that when God meets with an individual, if the individual has any contact with the powers of darkness, God's meeting with that person or group will break the powers of darkness of that person or group.

Martin Luther once made a comment, "When I pray coincidences happen, when I don't pray, they don't." Chance happenings are very common in the Bible. They are only happenstance from man's view, but it was God's purpose directing the situation. Ruth when she came back with her mother in-law to Bethlehem Judah went straight to work. When she chose the field to work in, it was by chance she stepped into Boaz's field. This was by chance in man's view, but it was the hand of God directing her. She had no idea that Boaz would be her kinsman redeemer. She had no idea that her life was about to take a 180-degree turn. Yet when you walk in obedience to God, get ready to see some chance meetings.

Jacob is another person whose life was altered by a chance meeting. In Genesis 28, the story is recorded of Jacob's journey from Beersheba to Haran. On his journey as the sun was setting, he decided to take a break and rest. Verse 11 of the same chapter records, "So he came to a certain place and stayed there all night." The New King James uses the word, "certain place," while King James Version says "lighted upon." Both have the idea of a place happened upon. Jacob's plan was only to get some rest for a few hours and then move on. But God's plan was to change his nature, his life.

Maybe you—the reader—are in a chance place, but really it's a divine appointment. Let's say, you have a job working at a gas station. You are only doing this because you need money and you have bills to pay. You are thinking you'll do this for a few months so you can get on your feet and then look for a job that meets your educational qualifications or work interests. It's only a temporary stop. For Jacob, it was only a temporary stop. Yet God met with him and changed his life. In the same manner, who knows? This could be a divine appointment of God to work at a gas station. God might be having you work there because He wants to prepare you for owning your own business. I'm telling you, when you are following the leading of the Holy Spirit, you will have chance meetings, divine appointments.

Remember it's the person of the Holy Spirit working with you that creates chance meetings or divine appointments. It's chance in man's perspective, yet there are things planned by God that are coming your way.

The Holy Spirit began to use us to do the will of God even when we don't know how to go about it. Remember Romans 8:26-28, "Likewise the Spirit also helps in our weaknesses. For we do not know what we should pray for as we ought, but the Spirit Himself makes intercession for us with groanings which cannot be uttered. 27 Now He who searches the hearts knows what the mind of the Spirit is, because He makes intercession for the saints according to the will of God. 28 And we know that all things work together for good to those who love God, to those who are the called according to His purpose"

Intercessory prayer is warfare prayer. Many times in intercession you will have to attack, strike down, cut down, and destroy the works of the enemy. We do this to enforce the victory of Jesus. A perfect example would be the story of Joshua and the 5 kings of the Amorites. In this chapter 5 kings had come together to fight against the Gibeonites. Gibeonites called on Joshua for help as they had a covenant with Joshua and Israel. So Joshua went to help and defeated the armies, but the 5 kings fled and hid in a cave. Joshua found them and brought them out. It was time to kill them. The custom of victory was when the enemy (Leaders) were caught, that they were laid to the ground and the Winning Leader would put his feet on the necks/heads of the enemy and kill them. If you remember the story of David and Goliath, David when he knocked down Goliath with a stone, discovered that he didn't have a sword. So he quickly went over to Goliath, took his sword, put his feet upon his neck and cut his head off. As soon as the philistines saw this they fled. There was always a display of conquest. This is what is meant by Colossians 2:15 that Jesus made a public display of them, having triumphed over them through Him". So coming back to the story of Joshua; When Joshua caught these kings and laid them to the ground. Instead of him, putting his feet on the necks on the enemy, he calls for some of his soldiers and tells them to do it. This is a perfect picture painted for us to attack strike down, enforcing the victory. Jesus already defeated the devil, so in intercession we come against the enemy who is continually giving trouble, and enforcing the victory. As Joshua said to his soldiers, Jesus is saying to us, Enforce the victory of the cross — strike down, cut down, destroy, and enforcing victory our sickness, disease, sin, unrighteousness, temptations, etc. So intercession when someone is being attacked we step in and enforce the victory of Jesus and pull down the strongholds.

Romans 16:20 "And the God of peace will soon crush Satan under YOUR feet".

This aspect of Intercession has to do with carrying the burdens of others. Jesus was a great example of this. The Bible says that Sin was laid upon Him. It's our Sin that was laid upon Him and he carried it away, or bore it away. II Corinthians 5:21 says, "He made Him who knew no sin to be sin on our behalf, that we might become the righteousness of God in Him". The Bible commands us to bear up the weaknesses of other. Look at Galatians 6:1,2 "Brethren, if a man is overtaken in any trespass, you who are spiritual restore such a one in a spirit of gentleness, considering yourself lest you also be tempted. 2 Bear one another's burdens, and so fulfill the law of Christ."

One picture that comes to my mind is that of tag-team wrestling. When a person is in the ring and he is fighting his enemy. If he feels weak or incapable, he simply tags his team mate and the team mate comes in with fresh strength to fight. In the same manner, when a person is in fight, maybe it's against sickness, against temptations, etc, we are able to step in and take that fight through prayer, and that's Intercession. We've step between two parties.

So looking at the definitions, we understand that it's our privilege to respond to God's call to intercession. Intercession is an extension of Jesus' ministry, for the Bible says in Hebrews 7:25, "...He always lives to make intercession for them." Jesus is the greatest example to follow as an intercessor. He has stood between us, our sin, and Satan, and by His precious blood made the way open to the Father God. He identified with our sinfulness and took the sin of all generations and removed it through the work of the cross. The Church is a house of prayer for all nations. Watchman Nee, the great Chinese Bible scholar and leader, said "How is God's will to be done on earth? Only by...remember...that the Church at prayer is heaven's outlet, the channel of release for heaven's power, and that this ministry is our greatest work possible."

Intercession is the responsibility of every believer. Throughout history God has looked for people who will take upon themselves the responsibility of an intercessor. Isaiah 59:16, "He saw that there was no man, and wondered that there was no intercessor; therefore His own arm brought salvation for Him; and His own righteousness, it sustained Him." You will see the downfall of cities and nations where there are no intercessors. Even still today, the Church of Jesus lacks people who will take up such a responsibility. Of course, at times, great men and women embraced the responsibility and made history. In every generation, in every city, in every nation, God is seeking people who will embrace the ministry of intercession.

# Four Characteristics of an Intercessor

There is a story in Luke 11 that gives us a great picture of intercession. When the disciples came to Jesus and asked Him to teach them to pray, he tells us the principles of prayer like "Our Father," "Hallowed be thy name," "Forgive us", and then in conjunction with those principles, he tells them this story:

"And He said to them, 'Which of you shall have a friend, and go to him at midnight and say to him, "Friend, lend me three loaves; for a friend of mine has come to me on his journey, and I have nothing to set before him"; and he will answer from within and say, "Do not trouble me; the door is now shut, and my children are with me in bed; I cannot rise and give to you"? I say to you, though he will not rise and give to him because he is his friend, yet because of his persistence he will rise and give him as many as he needs. So I say to you, ask, and it will be given to you; seek, and you will find; knock, and it will be opened to you. For everyone who asks receives, and he who seeks finds, and to him who knocks it will be opened'" (Luke 11:5–10).

It is important to note the person who was going to feed the visitors knew where to get bread. He didn't frantically go to different houses. He knew which house to go to. In the same manner, it is important that we become aware of God's power and love for our lives. This changes the whole aspect of intercession. If we are in doubt of God's power, then our intercession is useless. There are 4 things to be noted in this story.

## Urgency

There was great urgency in getting the bread—the answer. The guests were already in the house. There is a wonderful verse I like in the book of Exodus. Moses was pleading with Pharaoh to let the Israelites go to worship. Pharaoh did not allow them to go. So the Lord God sent plagues to the land of Egypt, but this didn't affect the people of God. After some of these plagues, finally Pharaoh says, "Go but don't go very far and please intercede for me" (Exodus 8:28). If we opened our eyes and looked around, there is the same cry that is coming from our neighborhood, from our city, from our nation, "Please intercede for me" I want to tell you, you are living in times when the cry is getting louder, when there is increased urgency in the people. The Church has to respond in urgency and stand in the gap to pray—to intercede.

## Humility

Humility is an open acknowledgement of helplessness. Many times people don't receive anything from God because they don't humble themselves and acknowledge their helplessness. Remember, the way up is the way down. You have to humble yourself.

## Confidence

Confidence will be produced when we ask in the name of Jesus and pray according the Scriptures. "Now this is the confidence that we have in Him, that if we ask anything according to His will, He hears us" (1 John 5:14). "Beloved, if our heart does not condemn us, we have confidence toward God" (1 John 3:21).

## Perseverance

Keep knocking. He is not deterred by delay (9–10). Delay is never a denial. We have to learn to wait on God's timing and God's direction. The Bible says in Hebrews 6:12 "that you do not become sluggish, but imitate those who through faith and patience inherit the promises." This man got what he wanted—bread. Always remember there are rewards for intercession. The Bible says when Job interceded for his friend that he was restored all that he lost in double measure. "And the LORD restored Job's losses when he prayed for his friends. Indeed the LORD gave Job twice as much as he had before" (Job 24:10).

# Responsibilities of an Intercessor

We will look to the Scriptures to get insight into this concept of intercessory prayer. The Bible outlines five main responsibilities of an Intercessor.

## Reminding God of His Promises

An Intercessor is a person who reminds God of His promises and appointments yet to be met and fulfilled. The reminder is more like evidence taken to court for a case to be tried. "'I have set watchmen on your walls, O Jerusalem; they shall never hold their peace day or night. You who make mention of the LORD, do not keep silent, and give Him no rest till He establishes and till He makes Jerusalem a praise in the earth'" (Isaiah 62:6–7).

Please understand that God doesn't forget us or the promises He has made towards us. He doesn't forget His covenant with us for the Bible says that God is a covenant-keeping and covenant-revealing God. So why must we proclaim it? The reason we proclaim it is because there is power when we speak out the Word of God. The Bible says in Psalm 45:1 that your tongue is a like a pen. So you can use your tongue, with the ink of God's Word, you can write your destiny in accordance with God's purpose for your life.

When we are interceding for salvation on behalf of an unsaved person we need to proclaim with our mouths the desired result. Are there promises of God's Word that you haven't seen fulfilled in your life? Are there prophecies that don't seem to be fulfilled? Open your mouth and speak forth the Word of God till you see those things come to pass. Get some perseverance in your life. Make warfare. Paul encourages Timothy of doing the same thing, making warfare in 1 Timothy 1:18–19, "This charge I commit to you, son Timothy, according to the prophecies previously made concerning you, that by them you may wage the good warfare, having faith and a good conscience, which some having rejected, concerning the faith have suffered shipwreck." When you see promises in the Scriptures, make them personal. When it says you, change it to I or me and speak out the Word of God.

## Stands in the Gap

Ezekiel 22:30 says, "'So I sought for a man among them who would make a wall, and stand in the gap before Me on behalf of the land, that I should not destroy it; but I found no one.'" To stand in the gap is to mediate between two parties. Maybe you are standing in the gap for a city or a group of people; we begin to plead for mercy instead of judgment. We plead the Honor of God's name. We plead the power of the blood of Jesus. Moses is a perfect example of someone who stands in the gap. In Exodus 32, while Moses was called up to the top of the mountain to have a meeting with God, the children of Israel grew restless waiting for Moses. So they appointed their own leader, and made a calf out of gold, and worshipped it, saying, "This is our God, which has brought us out of Egypt." The Israelites had quickly forgotten the goodness of God. While on the mountain God says to Moses, go down and check on your people, for they are sinning, and tell them that He is going to kill them. Moses suddenly stands in the gap for the children of Israel. Let's read the story and then we will note couple of things.

> And the LORD said to Moses, "I have seen this people, and indeed it is a stiff-necked people! Now therefore, let Me alone, that My wrath may burn hot against them and I may consume them. And I will make of you a great nation." Then Moses pleaded with the LORD his God, and said: "Lord, why does Your wrath burn hot against Your people whom You have brought out of the land of Egypt with great power and with a mighty hand? Why should the Egyptians speak, and say, 'He brought them out to harm them, to kill them in the mountains, and to consume them from the face of the earth'? Turn from Your fierce wrath, and relent from this harm to Your people. Remember Abraham, Isaac, and Israel, Your servants, to whom You swore by Your own self, and said to them, 'I will multiply your descendants as the stars of heaven; and all this land that I have spoken of I give to your descendants, and they shall inherit it forever.'" So the LORD relented from the harm which He said He would do to His people (Exodus 32:9–14).

Here we find that Moses stood in the gap and pleaded with God for mercy on behalf of the Israelites. We find Moses pleaded with God for four things:

a. **Moses pleaded with God regarding His character** (verse 11). Moses told God that He would be out of character if He killed the Israelites after leading them triumphantly out of Egypt. As you've read in the verse above, you might be wondering how come God changed his mind. I thought God doesn't change! Please understand when the Bible says, God doesn't change, it means His character doesn't change. His character is consistent. He will always be a God of love, mercy, forgiveness. His character remains the same. Moses was simply pointing out to God about His character. He was saying in essence, "You knew that these people were not perfect when You brought them out, so why get angry at them now? Let's give them time to change."

b. **Moses sought the glory of God's name.** He reminded God that, if He didn't do this, all other nations would make fun of the Israelites and, in turn, make fun of God. He told God that this would give them reason to slander His name.

c. **Moses pleaded and reminded God of His covenant.** Moses reminded God that He had been faithful to Abraham, Issac, and Jacob, also noting they were people who made mistakes and sinned.

d. **Moses pleaded with God for mercy even if it cost him his life.** Exodus 32:32 reads, "'Yet now, if You will forgive their sin—but if not, I pray, blot me out of Your book which You have written.'" Can you believe this? Moses is saying, "Lord forgive them. But if you don't, then blot out my name also." Please understand we have this kind of authority in intercession. Look back to the beginning of this chapter at the opening quotation from Rees Howell. This is what he was talking about—identifying with the person or people for whom you are praying.

## Building a Hedge of Protection

An intercessor is a person who builds a hedge (wall) around a person, place, or nation. In Nehemiah 4, the people had a mind to help rebuild the walls around Jerusalem. These walls "were being restored and the gaps were beginning to be closed" (Nehemiah 4:7). We need to build walls of protections around people, to cover them in prayer.

I'm sure you've seen signs posted like "No Dumping allowed," "No Trespassing, violator will be prosecuted," "No parking," "No standing," etc. All these signs say one thing: don't cross the boundary. Spiritually speaking, we need to post signs around our lives, our churches, our cities, and our nations. We need signs like

"No trespassing," "No accidents," and "No harassment." We can post these signs through prayer. Once the signs are posted, the devil has to stay away. These signs serve as hedges of protection, walls of protection, and fences of protection.

Ezekiel 13:4–5 reads, "'O Israel, your prophets have been like foxes among ruins. You have not gone up into the breaches [breaks], nor did you build the wall [hedge] around the house of Israel to stand in the battle on the day of the Lord.'" In old times, the majority of the cities had walls around them for protection. Some of these walls were as thick as 24 feet. In the same manner, through prayer, we need to build protection–boundary lines. Many people blame God for accidents, destructions, etc. The problem is not God; it's our failure to build a hedge.

The Bible describes a person who doesn't have a hedge built around his life as:

- **Bitten by the serpent (devil)** — "He whose hedge is broken, the serpent will bite him" (Ecclesiastes 10:8).
- **Destroyed fruit** — "Why have You broken down her hedges, so that all who pass by the way pluck her fruit?" (Psalm 80:12).
- **Strongholds of Satanic power** — "You have broken down all his hedges; You have brought his strongholds to ruin" (Psalm 89:40).

## Filling the Cup of God's Blessing

An intercessor is a person who through prayer and fasting fills the cup of God's blessing to overflowing. Revelation 5:8 tells us, "Now when He had taken the scroll, the four living creatures and the twenty-four elders fell down before the Lamb, each having a harp, and golden bowls full of incense, which are the prayers of the saints." Psalm 75:8 tells us of another type of bowl or cup, "For in the hand of the LORD there is a cup, and the wine is red; it is fully mixed, and He pours it out; surely its dregs shall all the wicked of the earth drain and drink down." These two cups are the cup of the prayers of the saints and the cup of iniquity.

The Bible paints a picture of these two cups to represent the blessing or judgment to be poured on a person. The picture would seem something like this: over every person there are these two cups, over every family, over every church, over every city, and over every nation. Whichever cup we fill will be poured out on us, our churches, our cities, and our nations. Our acts of the carnal nature fill the cup of iniquity. Our prayers, fasting, confession of God's Word, mercy, shared love of Jesus—these things fill the cup of God's blessing.

## Obeying Jesus' Command to Watch and Pray

Jesus commanded His disciples who were accompanying Him, "'Watch and pray, lest you enter into temptation. The spirit indeed is willing, but the flesh is weak'" (Matthew 26:41). An intercessor is a person who obeys the command of Jesus to watch and pray. The word watch occurs 11 times in the three Gospels accounts of Matthew 24, Mark 13, and Luke 21—the prophecy chapters. To watch means to be on alert, to be on the lookout. Watchmen are still common today in most nations. The job of the watchman is to stay awake all night to protect the place from danger or any intruders. In Bible times, almost every city had watchmen not only for the night but also for the day. This job was 24 hours a day. The job of watchman was to be on the lookout for any visitors. If he saw someone coming from afar, he would send one person to meet with the person and find out his purpose for coming before he was allowed to come any closer. If the watchman sensed danger, he would alarm the entire city, and the city would be ready to defend itself. We need to watch similarly over our families, churches, cities, and nations. We need to see with God's eyes any signs of danger or intruders, and alarm believers to get in their places.

As we have looked at so many aspects of Spiritual warfare, I pray that this book has stirred up your spirit and you have become hungry to know the principles of God to live a prevailing life in this world. May God continue to add grace to your life.

For more information about Pastor Nicky S. Raiborde, other audio and videos resources, please contact,

Fresh Focus Media,
A division of International Family Church
1311 Marley Drive,
Columbia, SC 29210
Tel. 803.731.0089

http://www.daniel1132.com
ifcsc@hotmail.com

Printed in the United States
150217LV00003B/81/P